Dan Secklemann

RETURN OF THE WHITE WHALE

This book is dedicated to Ruth and Richard Yardumian

 www.trafford.com

North America & international
toll-free: 1 888 232 4444 (USA & Canada)
fax: 812 355 4082

CONTENTS

Artists:

Whale on cover: Andra King
Inside Portraits: Julio Espiritis

INTRODUCTION

MELVILLE'S NOVEL, MOBY DICK is an allegorical tale riding beside a true episodic human story of a people's history and their presence today; their monumental accomplishments, their power and their madness.

Moby Dick acts as a matrix, a "stand-alone" story for the reader to savor parabolic significances. I have given the full story minus many of the author' rhetorical flights. Where Melville's words shouldn't be eliminated nor matched, I quote him. Any student required to review Moby Dick will find it here, concise and easy reading. Further, there are "mini-bios" herein that can be studied, a small way toward our comprehending the debt we owe to a long maligned people.

Early on, I blend some personal family history into the narrative. It is relevant. On my paternal side my forbearers belonged to the continuing "Diaspora". I mention my father and mother's backgrounds for balance. There are references to my personal experiences, where they relate to the topic.

Moby Dick and my account trade places frequently and mostly without a literary bridge. In a sense you will be reading two stories at the same time; and yet, both may reach the same conclusion.

CHAPTER ONE

CALL ME ISHMAEL

CALL ME ISHMAEL...SO BEGINS Herman Melville's novel, *Moby-Dick*, a whaling saga steeped in irony and allegory. It is also a primer on life aboard a whaler; an adventure, but it also describes the lot of the crew: of hard work, cramped conditions, sweat, noises and odors that was all part of life on those sailing vessels.

A young man, Ishmael takes the reader on board as he acts as the narrator. It is a compelling yarn, even when he details the rendering oil extraction processes and boiling blubber, and other times when when he waxes about the parts of the ship, the crew, whales and harpoons.

The name Ishmael is from the Bible, the Old Testament. It is the name of a child born to the maid-servant, Hagar, and Abraham. Abraham's wife, (Sarai) Sarah, later has them expelled into the desert. Yet he survives to become the founder of great nations.

Call me Joseph Daniel, I have two biblical names and I'm a survivor of sorts, I'm 81 years old and married 57 years, father of 5 splendid offsprings, 7 grandchildren, and one great grand child. I served in the Navy in the Pacific during WWII. My father's father, Siegmund Charles Seckelmann, was a Jew who married a Christian woman from a family named Bowditch. My grandfather came to this country as a child from Bavaria with his mother and father sometime in 1840's. When he was 19 and the Civil War had begun, he enlisted in the Fifth N.Y. Volunteers. He was wounded, recovered and remained in the war and went through many battles. When it was learned that he was also a musician he was assigned to the regimental band. He was an enlisted man. After the war he married and settled in Bethlehem Pa. where he was active in the civic and cultural life of the community. He became an officer in the Pennsylvania Militia, was an organizer of a Choral Society that featured the works of J.S. Bach and Felix Mendlesohn. Around this time he became the Fire Chief of Bethlehem. He was father to six children. My father was the youngest.

My father received schooling in Bethlehem in part through the Moravian Church. His father, Civil War Veteran and fire chief, died in 1900. My father, then just 14 years old, went to work for Bethlehem Steel, was apprenticed to an electrician. By the time he was 17 he decided to join the Navy. His mother had to give her permission. In time he was assigned to the USS Rhode Island, one of the ships of The Great White Fleet of Teddy Roosevelt. In his diary he tells of the time Roosevelt came aboard, gave a speech, dined with the men, even took a turn in the Black-Gang shoveling coal. Earlier my father had entered the Navy Medical Corps. Here he became a dedicated student. Later the Navy sent him to Yale. During the first World War he achieved war time rank of Lt. Commander. He was a pioneer in the use and interpretation of X-rays and clinical testing in military medicine. He had married my mother just as she graduated from the Nursing School of a Philadelphia hospital.

My mother, Annie Wharton, was the second child of James Wharton born in the United States. The Baldwin Locomotive Works in Philadelphia brought skilled railroad artisans from England. It was said that he could build a complete locomotive from the ground up. One brother, George, became an Episcopal Minister, and in retirement in Phoenix, Arizona when I visited him in the 1960's he was Chaplin for the States Assembly.

I feel I have a literary kinship with Melville's narrator, the 19th century, and, for that matter, with biblical names. Ishmael, Joseph and Daniel, all in The Old Testament, had been abused, only to be raised to great stature. The humble Ishmael of Melville's book and I just survive to tell a story.

The book begins in New Bedford with Ishmael meeting and befriending a harpooner, an aboriginal named Quequeg, who was trying to sell a shrunken head. They go to Nantucket where they both sign on a whaling ship, The Pequod... As they make their way in Nantucket they are confronted by a man who appears as an apparition with bedraggled clothes, pocked skin and glaring eyes he asks,... "Have you shipped on?" He then utters a cryptic, fretful warning of doom to follow the captain... Capt. Ahab and the ship, The Pequod. Then the stranger says his name is, Elijah!

The biblical Elijah and his successor as prophets of The Almighty confound evil King Ahab. Ahab was the King of Israel but had turned to idol worship of Baal and as such... "Now Ahab son of Omri did evil in the sight of the Lord, more than all who were before him"...(Kings 1-17/30)

Capt. Ahab is shown as an able mariner and capable, though odd and puzzling. He has a pathological fixation on the destruction of an oversized white whale...Moby Dick. In an earlier encounter with that leviathan it cost him the loss of a leg and the morbid altering of his psyche. To his crew he is an enigmatic force, pacing the quarterdeck with an uneven cadence produced by the peg leg fashioned from the bone of a whale, thumping against the deck planking.

He ruminates his deep hurt and hate.

Capt. Ahab in Melville's 19th century nautical story depicts the consequences of a festering victim complex. In our time we see this, but now the pain and suffering occurred to some ancestors, and the descendants never cease screaming that they are owed continuous redress, and the more society acquiesces, the more demanding they become. Yet, there are some causes this day for real pain from discrimination and other evils.

When my great grandfather Charles Jacob Seckelmann came to this country from Bavaria he was a classical painter, an artist whose works graced both Churches and Temples. When commissions were scarce, to support his family he'd paint signs for merchants and municipalities. He was fluent in five European languages.

He and his contemporaries and those that followed enriched our country. If their leaving the Old World left a void, it was rarely noticed, nor were their talents appreciated. Of course the Old World was poorer for it.

During the 19th century and through the early part of the 20th century there was a great migration of Europeans to America. Many of the immigrants have made lasting contributions to our culture and well being. Of those, the Jews have and still are having the greatest impact. Most has been for good, but not all. Also there are some intriguing statistics we should note about them and the rest of the U S population:

(Fig. Extrapolated from 2000 census)

Est. Population U S =282.5 million

Jews

    2% Approx. 5,500,000

Afro. Am

    12.4% Approx. 35,500,000

Hispanic

    13% Approx. 37,200,000

Asian

    4% Approx. 11,000,000 (including Asian, Native American, Alutes)

Caucasian (All)

    75% Approx. 210,000,000

CHAPTER TWO

COMING ABOARD

ELIJAH WARNS ISHMAEL WITH Quequeg again as they're about to board the Pequod. He asks if they'd seen men boarding the ship Ishmael says he saw them. Then Elijah says, "See if you can find them now...?"

Capt. Ahab does not make his appearance for several days after the ship gets underway. Then Ishmael sees him standing, and notices a white scar running down the side of his face and continuing beyond inside his garments, and that one of his legs is a white peg, and that he steadied from the pitching motion of the ship by placing the peg leg into a hole augered into the deck.

Ishmael does not see the men Elijah referred to, but remembers them when they came aboard almost as shadows. Several months into the voyage he then finds that they are not phantoms, but were of eastern origin, from the Manillas, as was their leader named Fedallah, also called the Parsee. He is Ahab's harpooner and confidant.

Ahab has 3 Mates each is aware of their Captain's obsession:

Chief Mate, Starbuck, a native of Nantucket. Besides his professional abilities, he has dignity, courage and a sense of duty. His courage and bravery are all in play against physical terrors, but he is not able to oppose Ahab's mania-driven cunning.

2nd Mate, Stubb who lives for the moment, and hunts whales for the excitement. He has no philosophy of any social conscience, and therefore no strong reason to oppose Ahab.

3rd Mate, Flask is mediocre and as 3rd Mate is least qualified to oppose Ahab.

The rest of the crew came from all parts of the globe, suggesting the Pequod as a ship is symbolic of the world.

Each of the Mates picks a Harpooner:

Starbuck selects, Queequeg (Ishmael's friend).

Stubb selects, Tashego, a New England Indian.

Flask selects, Daggoo, a huge coal-black African.

So important are the harpooners that their social status is up close to the officers. Their parallels today would be athletes. They are given great respect. Society always needs champions, and the closed microcosm of a whaling ship doesn't lack any. Where and when they eat and sleep on the vessel always takes in account their positions.

In Capt. Ahab's near total absorption, his monomania for the destruction of Moby-Dick, he has assembled his weaponry, his army, committing the Pequod, his world to war. He is not so insane as to not permit the ship to take other whales on the way so as to placate the crew who'd share in the oil profits. He entreats the crew to join him in his quest. He produces an ounce gold coin as a prize for the first man to sight the great white whale with the crooked jaw and three holes in its starboard fluke. He tells the crew that the Pequod will sail from the end of one ocean to another in search of Moby-Dick. He brings out wine twice and the flagon is passed in a ceremony dedicated to the destruction of Moby-Dick. The crew cheers the announcement. But 1st Mate Starbuck is silent. Later he tells Ahab that only the captains' retribution will be served and that hunting whales for oil is the ship's first duty, and not hunting Moby-Dick for the commander's vengeance.

CHAPTER THREE

WHERE ARE WE?

THE STRIKING STATISTICS IN AMERICA of the accomplishments of a very small segment of our population is a great wonder. Of the Jews, even without their biblical history as God's chosen, one could say within them exists an extraordinary gene pool. But their creative interests include more than science, more than the arts; it also includes expressions of love of country, and of all mankind.

Harvey Sarner, a friend of mine, has written a book on the Righteous Gentiles. The book deals with people in occupied Europe during the Holocaust who at extreme personal risk sheltered Jews without hope of reward. For the most part they were not what you'd call especially trained nor equipped for the hero's role to do what they did, but when other humans were at risk they prevailed.

Over our history in America and throughout the world there are myriad examples of Righteous Jews; some are gifted musicians, scientists, teachers, physicians, writers, inventors, industrialists, financers, engineers, physicist or they may be taxi drivers, contractors, athletes, publishers, entertainers, and even lawyers. It might even include judges and elected office holders. At the time of this writing (the figures will fluctuate from year to year), 7% of the U.S. Congress people are Jews. Eleven percent in the Senate and 7.9% of the House, coming from 34 of our 50 states. That 2 to 2¼ percent of the population is amply represented in national, state and local judiciaries and law making bodies. The statement does not mean that they are not representing the interests of all the people.

The temptation within all professions to put forth one's own agenda is greatest with those who work in media: TV, Movies, Recording, Publishing. When a consumer engages media they are submitting to a benign form of hypnotism. In the case of TV – Audio-visual for many, it ceases to be benign. The power is more than awesome. Advertisers pay millions of dollars for less than a minute for exposure on a high profile event, and watching – listening for any length of time, the consumer and his children will know what's cool to do, to buy, who to vote for... whether aberrant sex is now normal (cool), whether marriage is necessary, or whether it can include the same sex unions. Awesome indeed. Witness how a shameless pervert shredded the Ten Commandments, then with the help of the Media-Moguls and rich entertainers became a two-term president.

One wonders if those influencing or controlling the audio-visual media ever encountered a great leviathan that tore off a leg and are they now hobbling around with a peg leg shaped from the bones of a whale? ... Are they seeking the destruction of that great white whale? Maybe they are. Or if not, why do they manipulate, alter, pervert, denigrate, what is left of a Moral-Consensus by lobbing subtle but insidious harpoons masquerading as humor, complete with electronic laughter and applause.

It "primes our pumps," to generate the mood of lighthearted acceptance. Strangely, when they produce a wholesome movie/video, the bottom line mostly indicates a financial success. Money can't be the motivation to create trash.

Interesting Statistics from US 2000 census:

Radio Stations: 4,760 AM and 5,542 FM

T.V. Stations: more than 1,500 of these 1,000 are affiliates of NBC-ABC-CBS-FOX or PBS.

Cable T.V. Stations: 9,000

We say, "They" are doing this or that. Who are the, "They". Well, "They," the Media, are 90% owned or controlled by a segment of the tiny minority that has had the greatest impact on us. "Impact" is a mild word. In fact we are in the process of our society being "re-sculptured." Some of their influence has resulted in good. Today's media has brought black people and all minorities into the mainstream, no longer portraying them as servile simpletons but equals. However, that good is overshadowed by radar–guided media-harpoons, and we human cetaceans must join their circus, die, or find an inaccessible redoubt with no electricity.

It is impossible to raise children free from their influences. You can install double locks on the doors, get a security system, have break-proof windows, and motion detectors, etc. but that will not stop these thieves from stealing the innocence of your children right in the Living Room, even while you're in the house. It is done not by a big bang, but incrementally. Each "insult" –laugh, is followed by another that tops the previous. Continued on this diet, in time the insults are passé. What had been aberrant, immoral, disgusting behavior is evolving as "normal and acceptable," even "cool." Those disagreeing are demoted to prudes, religious fanatics or poor souls who must have been mentally short-changed.

CHAPTER FOUR

JOIN THE NAVY & THE OPINION MAKERS

Author @ 17 years old

WHEN I WAS 17 YEARS OLD (my father died when I was 11 years old) with my mother's permission I joined the Navy on January 2, 1941. I left Philadelphia and in the dead of winter went to Newport, Rhode Island for boot camp. It was rigorous training in severe weather and my 6 ft. 168 lb. frame went down to 143 lbs. It was there I saw other recruits at the bidding of their peers empty the sea-bag, and a hammock of a young recruit-sailor into the showers as well as his person, forcing him to scrub all with salt-water-soap because someone said he was a dirty Jew. At the same time in our barracks a 6'3" monster "Christian," with filthy nails and an odor to match wasn't touched.

Later, after finishing Boot Camp, I was sent to Hospital Corp School at the Naval Hospital by the Brooklyn Navy Yard, New York. I was a bit emaciated from the loss of weight. One morning after having been there about 10 days I had a shaking experience. I was in the Head (toilet) when a burley fellow student, an older guy about 32 years who was about my height but weighed over 200 lbs. came in. He asked me what I thought about the idea of his regarding one of our classes, and I answered as a tactless teenager saying I thought it was dumb. With that and no warning he cuffed me on the side of the head, knocking me off the toilet onto the floor saying, "No Jew boy is going to talk to me like that." I had no strength to fight the brute. I mumbled that I was a Protestant, "You gotta Jew name." I had to endure his presence until graduation. If I, who had a some what cherubic-Gaelic continence had to suffer because of my last name, I was sure that real Jews would carry more scars. We weren't at war at the time but I knew we'd be fighting the Nazis soon. The presence of "shipmates" like him and others makes one quake and ponder.

This much we know, Ishmael says, "Moby Dick", the Great White Whale, was a symbol of the world's evils to Captain Ahab, and had to be destroyed.

The slights, insults, degradations, pain and murders inflicted on Jews over the centuries have been awful, but that was before today's forms of mass media. It was before they realized the genesis of their troubles... "Opinion!" Opinions were always controlled and disseminated by others while they tried to work in their trades, worship their God, raise their children, etc. only to be persecuted by the minions of the Opinion Makers... Now Opinion Making belongs to them...

That statement may seem simplistic, because Jews have been in some form of media for centuries. In the year 1526, two brothers of a famous Jewish family, the Kohens, were printers in Bohemia. In this country some of the great Jewish fortunes were made in the publishing and at the start of the 20th century, in the motion picture industries. However, early on, Jewish ownership was rare and insular. In the recent past, it was more diverse and those in media were restrained by local and general mores, authorities and the state of art. Today's technology and the liberal interpretation of law assures that salacious media messages permeate our every corpuscle.

Today the opinions of the non-Jew had a "Sea-Change." It has occurred in my lifetime, caused in no small part by the media orchestration. There are still small pocket prejudices but they're generally isolated. Might they be re-ignited and spread by the great winds of disgust?

The good that has resulted from their husbandry of the media can crash as citizens see the deluge of deviant sex, unnecessary mayhem and political correctness that is corrupting their values and families.

The questions are: Are the Opinion Makers punishing society for past sins? Or are they largely controlled by evil, depraved amoral beings who just crave more company?

Should the useful citizen and his family totally succumb to the media morality, chaos and dysfunction could take over. Who would fly our jets, design the computers and software, man our subs, tend the satellites, etc... I'm sure the Opinion Makers are thanking ...something...for the brave Navy and Air Force Pilots and all Service Personnel in response to the 9/11/01 atrocity.

"THE CONSCIENCE OF CHILDREN IS FORMED BY THE INFLUENCES THAT SURROUND THEM; THEIR NOTION OF GOOD AND EVIL ARE THE RESULT OF THE MORAL ATMOSPHERE THEY BREATHE."

-Richter

CHAPTER FIVE

GAMS, WHALES, SEAMAN'S CHAPEL

USUALLY WHEN ONE WHALE-SHIP crosses the path of another they stop, exchange pleasantries and sometimes mail. This was called a "Gam." Capt. Ahab always called, "Have ye seen the White Whale?" If the answer is the negative, he cuts the Gam short, but if they had, he would linger to find more. He learned that those who had an encounter with Moby-Dick paid a high price. A mounting list of calamities were related:

First Mate of the Jeroboam, killed;

Capt. Of the Samuel Elderly lost an arm;

Total whaleboat crew including the Captain's son of the whaler Rachel, lost;

Five men from the whaler, Delight, killed;

Desertion by the crew of the Town-Ho because a harpooner was devoured.

Hitler played the Victim-Card, blaming the punitive Treaty of Versailles and the Jews for Germany's problems. Victimhood is the greatest vehicle for a scoundrel to initiate control. Germany's suffering parlayed Hitler to the pinnacle of power and evil madness. And it all ended after the death of millions and loathsome atrocities and destruction.

Staring at Hitler's picture long enough, some can see that he could have had a peg-leg fashioned from the bone of a whale.

Ishmael continues to educate the reader when he points out that there are two types of whales hunted by men. He says that the nobler of the two is the Sperm Whale, a toothed whale, and the other is the Right Whale. The toothed one has one blowhole and the other has two. He continues about the whale's anatomy, even where you can find a great reservoir of oil in the Sperm Whale's head. He also notes that the Sperm Whale eyes are on the opposite sides of its head and must be seeing two sets of images and is able to process them. In a homey way, Melville has Ishmael make insightful observations throughout the story...Ishmael's friend Queeqeuq as a harpooner has to cut up the killed whales when they are lashed to the side of the vessel. There is always danger of slipping off and falling among the sharks into their feeding frenzy as they tear at the dead whale, but Queequeq is tied to another seaman who is on the ship by the "Monkey-Rope-Of-The-Life." It is Ishmael who is tethered to keep Queequeq from harm. The comradeship between Ishmael and Queeqeuq is extended to imply that all men survive by being joined together by some type of bond.

Let us briefly go back to the time when Ishmael and Queeqeuq first met: Ishmael arrives at the Sprouter-Inn in New Bedford in freezing weather looking for a night's lodging. The Inn Keeper, Mr. Coffin, has Ishmael reluctantly share sleeping accommodations with a "Harpooner." He doesn't tell Ishmael much about the harpooner; that perhaps he is a tattooed, aboriginal cannibal.

After some fright Ishmael finds his roommate quite civil though different. In spite of this he has a peaceful night's sleep and he observes... "That it is better to be with a sober cannibal than with a drunken Christian." They become friends and pledge to defend one another against all perils. Queeqeuq discloses that he is the son of the King of the Kokoroko Island in the South Pacific. When a whaling ship visits his island for water and provisions, he joins the crew by coming aboard at a narrow as the vessel is already underway on its way out to sea. The Captain of the ship was not pleased, but permitted him to stay on. In time he became an expert harpooner. Queeqeuq said that he was not ready to return, and became King.

Although at this time Ishmeal hadn't signed-on to any ship it was the custom for whale-men who were passing through New Bedford to pay a call at The Whalemen's Chapel especially if they were going to sea for 3 years. Ishmael was alone as he entered the Chapel. As his eyes adjusted to the diminished light he saw many memorial tablets with black borders cemented to the wall. Two of such said the following:

SACRED TO THE MEMORY OF JOHN TALBOT

who at the age of 18 lost overboard off
Patagonia & Isle of Desolation Nov, 1, 1836
This tablet erected to his memory by his sister

SACRED TO THE MEMORIES OF ROBERT LONG, WILLIS ELLERY, NAT COLEMAN, SETH MACY AND SAM GLEIG

Boat crew to the Ship Eliza

Towed out of sight by a whale in the Pacific Dec, 31, 1839
This marble placed by their shipmates

To Ishmael's surprise, he finds that Queequeg is sitting among the congregation and joins him. Soon the famous Father Mapple enters. He removes his sleet-covered outer garments and slowly climbs to his high pulpit by a rope ladder. As a young man, before going into the ministry, he had been a harpooner. His pulpit was shaped like the prow of a ship, at the top of which rested the Holy Bible. Upon opening his service he would address the Congregation as, "Shipmates"...

The sermon is on Jonah and the Whale and Repentance... "We must obey God and not ourselves... otherwise it could mean being swallowed up by our own folly ...by doing our own and not God's Will; which must result in our destruction."

Ishmael is moved by the sermon. He may have cause to harken back to it after he comes under Ahab's will. The atmosphere, the sermon, the memorial tablets contribute to Ishmael revealing his spiritual side to the readers when he says, "Me thinks we have hugely mistaken this matter of Life and Death. Me thinks that what they call my shadow here on earth is my true substance... Me thinks my body is the less of my better being. In fact take my body, who will. Take I say it is not me"

THEY THAT DENY GOD DESTROY A MAN'S NOBILTY; FOR CERTAINLY MAN IS KIN TO THE BEASTS BY HIS BODY, AND IF HE IS NOT AKIN TO GOD BY HIS SPIRIT, HE IS A BASE AND IGNOBLE CREATURE.

Bacon

The next morning Ishmael and Queequeg rent a wheelbarrow to carry their belongings. The shrunken head was sold to the local barber. They each paid the Innkeeper and made their way to the "Moss", a little Nantucket Packet-Schooner that would take them to Nantucket and the adventures ahead. On the way Queequeg does an heroic deed by saving a passenger who fell overboard from freezing and / or drowning by quickly diving after him and bringing him to safety. This occurred after the same fool had taunted Queequeg because of his appearance.

CHAPTER SIX

CHARLTON HESTON SPEECH

Back To Our Century

Charlton Heston

"YOU SIMPLY ......DISOBEY" from Wash. Times and 3/22/99 and others by Charlton Heston. The speech has been disseminated widely in many publications; Rush Limbaugh read it on the air & mailed it to thousands.

Charlton Heston spoke on the topic, "Winning the Cultural War," at the Harvard Law School Forum, February 16, 1999. The following text is reprinted with permission of the National Rifle Association: (Wash. Times)

I remember my son, when he was 5, explaining to his kindergarten class what his father did for a living. "My daddy," he said, "pretends to be people." There have been quite a few of them. Prophets from the Old and New Testaments, a couple of Christian saints, generals of various nationalities and different centuries, several kings, three American presidents, a French cardinal and two geniuses, including Michelangelo.

If you want the ceiling repainted I'll do my best. There always seem to be a lot of different fellows up here. I'm never sure which one of them gets to talk. Right now, I guess I'm the guy.

As I pondered our visit tonight it struck me: If the Creator gave me the gift to connect you with the hearts and minds of those great men, then I want to use that same gift now to reconnect you with your own sense of liberty...your own freedom of thought...your own compass for what is right. Dedicating the memorial at Gettysburg, Abraham Lincoln said of America, "We are now engaged in a great Civil War, testing whether this nation or any nation so conceived and so dedicated can long endure."

Those words are true again. I believe that we are again engaged in a great civil war, a cultural war that's about to hijack your birthright to think and say what resides in your heart.

I've worked with brilliantly talented homosexuals all my life. But when I told an audience that gay rights should extend no further than your rights or my rights, I was called a homophobe.

I served in World War II against Axis powers. But during a speech, when I drew an analogy between singling out innocent Jews and singling out innocent gun owners, I was called ante-Semite.

Everyone I know knows I would never raise a closed fist against my country. But when I asked an audience to oppose this cultural persecution, I was compared to Timothy McVeigh.

From Time magazine to friends and colleagues, they're essentially saying, "Chuck, how dare you speak your mind. You are using language not authorized for public consumption!"

But I am not afraid. If Americans believed in political correctness, we'd still be King George's boys-subjects bound to the British crown.

In New Jersey, despite the death of several patients nationwide who had been infected by dentists who had concealed their AIDS – the state commissioner announced that health providers who are HIV -positive need not... need not... tell their patients that they are infected. At William and Mary, students tried to change the name of the school team "The Tribe" because it was supposedly insulting to local Indians, only to learn that authentic Virginia chiefs truly like the name.

In San Francisco, city fathers passed an ordinance protecting the rights of transvestites to cross-dress on the job, and for transsexuals to have separate toilet facilities while undergoing sex change surgery.

In New York, kids who don't speak a word of Spanish have been placed in bilingual classes to learn their three R's in Spanish solely because their last names sound Hispanic.

At the University of Pennsylvania, in a state where thousands died at Gettysburg opposing slavery, the president of that college officially set up segregated dormitory space for black students.

Finally just last month (January)... David Howard, head of the Washington D.C. Office of public Advocate, used the word "niggardly" while talking to colleagues about budgetary matters. Of course, "niggardly" means stingy or scanty. But within days Howard was forced to publicly apologize and resign.

As columnist Tony Snow wrote: "David Howard got fired because some people in public employ were morons who (a) didn't know the meaning of 'niggardly,' (b) didn't know how to use a dictionary to discover the meaning, and (c) actually demanded that he apologize for their ignorance."

A few years back I heard about a rapper named Ice-T who was selling a CD called "Cop Killer" celebrating ambushing and murdering police officers. None other than Time/Warner, the biggest entertainment conglomerate in the world, was marketing it. Police across the country were outraged. Rightfully so- at least one had been murdered. But Time/Warner was stonewalling because the CD was a cash cow for them, and the media were tiptoeing around it because the rapper was black. I heard Time/Warner had a stockholders meeting scheduled in Beverly Hills. I owned some shares at the time. So I decided to attend.

What I did there was against the advice of my family and colleagues. I asked for the floor. To a hushed room of a thousand average American stockholders, I simply read the full lyrics of "Cop Killers" – every vicious, vulgar, instructional word.

> *I got my 12 gauge sawed off*
> *I got my headlights turned off*
> *I'm about to bust some shots off*

I'm about to dust some cops off

It got worse, a lot worse. I won't read the rest of it to you. But trust me, the room was a sea of shocked, frozen, blanched faces.

The Time/Warner executives squirmed in their chairs and stared at their shoes. They hated me for that. Then I delivered another volley of sick lyric brimming with racist filth, where Ice-T fantasizes about sodomizing two 12-year-old nieces of Al and Tipper Gore.

She pushed her butt against my...

Well, I won't do to you here what I did to them. Let's just say I left the room in echoing silence. When I read the lyrics to the waiting press corps, one of them said, "We can't print that." "I know," I replied, "but Time/ Warner is selling it." Two months later Time/Warner terminated Ice-T's contract. I'll never be offered another film by Warners, or get a good review from Time magazine. But disobedience means you must be willing to act, not just talk.

If you note the date of Mr. Heston's speech, Feb. 16, 1999 you'll see that Time/Warner until that time were in no hurry to make changes, even though another celebrity went after them for the same thing. William Bennet, the former Secretary of Education and the author of several best selling books as Co-Director of Empower America in 1995, in a letter to members of Empower America requested that the members sign a petition to the two top officers at Time/Warner to, "Take Responsibility." Further he says: "In addition to the powerful petition drive, I want to continue to run our television advertisement drawing attention to the issue. In that commercial, I asked Time/Warner to have one of its executive officers publicly read some of the lyrics we've reprinted here. They wouldn't do it. Enclosed with that letter was a separate sheet with the words from six of their "songs." They are crude and filthy. Their effect on our youth could shunt many a young buyer toward the bestial underclass that created them. Maybe that was what they wanted?"

CHAPTER SEVEN

RIGHTEOUS JEWS BIOS BEGIN

And Balak said unto Balaam,
What hast thou done unto me?
I took thee to curse mine enemies,
And behold thou hast blessed them
Bountifully!

Numbers 23-11

THE FOLLOWING IS THE FIRST of several mini-biographies of my notion of Righteous Jews. It is not at all an exhaustive search; that might fill a library to do the subject justice, but these are my candidates because I like what I see. Some are living contemporaries. The paint may be still wet and their final portrait is not finished.

> People who love the neighbor as themselves experience the delight of charity in the exercise of it, or in Uses. The life of charity is a life of Uses. Such life pervades the whole of heaven, for the Lord's Kingdom, being a Kingdom of mutual love, is a Kingdom of Uses.

> EMANUEL SWEDENBORG
> Arcana Caelestia #997

JULIUS ROSENWALD

Merchant Prince   Citizen Prince

Born in Springfield, IL. 1862, in a house across the street from where A. Lincoln once lived, to Augusta and Samuel Rosenwald.

As an adult he started his career in N.Y., then relocated to Chicago where he ran a store specializing in men's fashions. He joined Sears Roebuck & Co. as V.P. (1895-1910), Pres. (1910-1925) Chairman of the Board (1925-1932) helping the company grow to America's largest retail and catalog enterprise. He created one of the first savings and profit sharing plans for employees. He set up the Julius Rosenwald Fund, for the "well-being of mankind."

He gave to Jewish causes: The Jewish theological Seminary ofAmerica, The Hebrew Union College of Cincinnati, Jewish Charities of Chicago. He did not restrict his philanthropy to Jews; he helped feed hungry children in Germany after the first World War, helped establish colleges in Syria and Istanbul. Many Chicago citizens are grateful for the Museum of Science and Industry. Not all are aware that he built it and gave it to the city.

Possibly the best use he put his money to was when he teamed with his friend Booker T. Washington and their philosophies merged. They were both convinced that charity (alms-giving) would not relieve the black poverty, but that vocational training, basic and higher education would. With that in mind he set out to building schools for blacks in many parts of the rural south where they were badly needed. Self-help was the key, and he insisted that the receiving communities match his money with labor, materials and, where possible, funds. From 1917 until his death in 1932 over 5350 schools were built. Along with that he built YMCA-YWCA buildings for blacks throughout the country.

He was married, father of five children, widowed and married a second time before his death.

NO RACE CAN PROSPER TILL IT LEARNS THAT THERE IS AS MUCH DIGNITY IN TILLING A FIELD AS IN WRITING A POEM.

Booker T. Washington

Righteous Jews biographies will continue after the following:

Moby Dick takes on many forms in our time. On the natural plain in Melville's novel he would fulfill his destiny cruising the oceans' seas, besting the likes of whaling ships and crews that may test him.

Today he may show up as a Charlton Heston and cause a "blush" to be heard around the world echoing from the Time/ Warner Board Room's lounge lizards' faces. Or he may have the persistent, penetrating force of The American Family Association as it musters like-minded citizens and religious organizations to energize this white aquatic apparition by urging protests where it hurts most, in the pocketbook; boycotting the sponsor's products and the source of the irritant, the Producers of the entertainment and their "products." William Bennet and his followers should be included with the above.

He may take other forms more sinister, reckless and counter-productive such as White Supremacist, terrorist and anti-Semite organizations.

CHAPTER EIGHT

MICHAEL EISNER

THE FOLLOWING DETAILS AND DEPICTS the "soiling" of what was a wholesome American Icon, primarily by one Michael Eisner. A quote from his biography, "If it's not growing, it's going to die.

He was born in Mt. Kisco, New York in 1942 into a wealthy family. While in college he worked as a page for NBC and later in programming before moving to ABC in 1966, where his "programming" Soap Operas and sitcoms helpe boast ABC's "viewership" above the other two networks. Next he moved to motion pictures, with Paramount taking them from last place to

Michael Eisner

first place with productions like Marathon Man and Raiders of the Lost Ark.

In 1984 at the request of Roy Disney, the nephew of founder, Walt Disney, Eisner was made Chairman and Chief Executive Officer. Eisner put his, "Grow or die," theory into play. He took Disney Co. from a corporation to an Empire; a Disney chain of retail stores began to open in shopping malls world wide; Theme Parks for Japan and Europe; tie-ins with productions and merchandise; syndication deals whereby TV networks could show Disney movie products; further production of 'adult' sitcoms i.e., Home Improvement and Ellen.

In time Disney camp included: The Disney Channel, Walt Disney TV, Touchtone TV, Miramax Films, Hyperion Books and Anaheim Mighty Ducks. By 1995 he crowned his career with the acquisition of (ABC) Capital Cities/ ABC for about $20 billion, giving Disney control of many TV stations and many more radio stations, cable channels, 7 newspapers and magazines plus lots more. At the onset he may have reached too far in expansion: Japan and Euro. Disney (France) looked like financial disasters at first. The Empire's other enterprises, ethical or otherwise, made lots of money.

In the year 2000 his estimated personal wealth was $600 million. He resides in Los Angeles with his wife and children.

As of this writing The Disney "Empire" can include: Walt Disney Brands (educational products, music, travel, lodging, etc.), Buena Vista Brands (video, movie distribution, television), Capital Cities/ABC Brands (TV, entertainment, news and sports), Touchtone Pictures, Hollywood Records, ESPN, A&E TV Network, Lifetime TV Network, Disney Publishing, Hyperion Press, Chilton Publishers, Baseball Team The L.A. Angels.

The following is a direct re-print that the American Family Association has distributed to its members:

Disney boycott fact sheet
Products, policies and practices

PRO-HOMOSEXUAL

• Disney has extended company health benefits to live-in partners of homosexual employees. (The policy does not cover unmarried heterosexual couples who live together.)

• Disney executives have served on the board of a powerful homosexual advocacy organization.

• Disney-owned ABC television network has been the leading promoter of homosexuality on prime time TV with shows such as **Ellen, Relativity** and **Spin City.**

• Disney-affiliated Storyline Entertainment produced the controversial 1995 made-for-TV homosexual rights propaganda movie **The Margarethe Cammermeyer Story.**

• Disney continues to host the huge "Gay and Lesbian Day at Walt Disney World." The event has spilled over into the larger Orlando area. During the event Disney allows some of its properties to be used for homosexual parties.

• Disney has helped underwrite fund raising events for homosexual activists organizations.

• In 1994 Disney hired avowed lesbian Lauren Lloyd to develop female and lesbian movies. She has since left the company.

• Elizabeth Birch, executive director of a powerful homosexual activist organization, said Eisner personally told her that 40% of Disney's employees are homosexual.

• Hyperion Press, a Disney-owned subsidiary, has published:
⇒ *Lettin' It All Hang Out*, the autobiography of RuPaul, a well-known "drag queen" transvestite) entertainer.
⇒ *Growing Up Gay*, written by three homosexual comedians.
⇒ *Out & About Gay Travels* series, a travel guide for homosexuals.

• Actors Ernie Sabella and Nathan Lane said that the characters they played (Timon, the meerkat, and Pumbaa, the wart hot) in **The Lion King** are "the first homosexual Disney characters ever to come to the screen..."
• **Chasing Amy** (Miramax) is about a man's pursuit of a lesbian.
• **Chicks in White Satin** (Hollywood Pictures) is a film about a lesbian couple who decide on a semitraditional "commitment celebration."

ANTI-CHRISTIAN

• **Dogma** (Miramax) is an outrageous blasphemous satire of the Catholic Church. Reporting on the upcoming movie, one Internet news service said: Disney and Miramax enjoy antagonizing Christians with blasphemy..." In an effort to distance itself from "Dogma," Disney is expected to sell the movie to an independent company formed by Miramax principals Harvey and Bob Weinstein.
• **Priest**, distributed by Disney's wholly-owned subsidiary Miramax, is a pro-homosexual movie which depicts five Catholic priests as dysfunctionals and blames their problems on Church teachings. One priest is a homosexual; a second an adulterer; a third an alcoholic; a fourth demented; and the fifth just plain mean and vicious.

• Disney CEO Michael Eisner and The Walt Disney Company are both donors to People For the American Way (PAW), a group whose stated goal is to "monitor and counter the divisive agenda of the Religious Right."

• Disney signed Martin Scorsese, the director the The Last Temptation of Christ, Casino, Taxi Driver and many other hard-edged films to a 4-year contract.

ANTI-FAMILY, ANTI-SOCIAL
• Disney subsidiary Touchstone Pictures has purchased the screen rights to Chippendales, an

unpublished book about the m⁻¹⁻ strip club dancing industry.

• Disney allowed Victor Salva to continue directing its film Powder, even after the company learned he was a convicted child molester.

• Kids (Miramax) was described by Daily Variety magazine as "one of the most controversial American movies ever made." According to Newsweek, "The film follows a number of barely pubescent looking boys and girls around New York City as they smoke pot, bait gays, beat a black man and engage in graphic sex." Under pressure Miramax formed an independent company to market and distribute the pornographic movie.

VIOLENCE

• Pulp Fiction (Miramax) is a seedy, hyper-violent movie that was first rated NC-17. Further editing gave it an R rating. Other ultra-violent films include Miramax Halloween and Scream slasher fi⹁ series.

ON SCREEN SEX AND NUDITY

• Color of Night (Hollywood Pictures), featured full frontal nudity.
• The Advocate (Miramax) is filled with nudity. The movie was NC-17 (formerly "X"), but on appeal (and after cutting out a 12-second sex scene) it was given an R.

VULGARITY

• Disney oversees programming decisions on E!Entertainment Television, a cable channel which airs The Howard Stern Show, a video version of the incredibly raunchy radio show.

• Clerks (Miramax), a black and white film about New Jersey convenience store clerks, was originally rated NC-17 because graphic and sexually expli language is woven throughout th⹁ film. On appeal, it was given an R rating.

American Family Association 23-A

CHAPTER NINE

THE MOUSE BETRAYED (REVIEW)

THE FOLLOWING IS DRAWN FROM *The American Family Association "Journal"- the Nov./Dec.1998 issue: an article by Ed Vitagliano.*

It is in part a review of a book titled, *"Disney, The Mouse betrayed,"* by a husband and wife team, Peter and Rochelle Schweizer, both are investigative journalists. They interviewed those both inside and outside Disney to get a glimpse into the true nature of the company. And the image is not pretty...Eisner's new willingness to push the envelope became clear in 1995 when Disney (Touchtone) decided to produce Down and Out in Beverly Hills. "We were immediately drawn to the project," he said, "even though we knew that it would surely earn an "R" rating, something Disney, even under its touchtone Label, had never before permitted."

It was a calculated leap away from the company's family oriented past. By producing a movie with foul language and explicit sex, Eisner said, "We sent a message that Disney was prepared to support talented film makers and make movies that dealt frankly with contemporary adult life."

The Schweitzers write that in1989 Disney became a full partner in a Pay-Per-View company called Viewers Choice, which in the 1990's has (changed) become a leader in producing Soft-Core Pornography to customers. While Viewers Choice initially ran mainstream Hollywood films, in 1993 the Pay-Per-View Company added "Hot Choice," which airs "adult" movies. The channel offers such fare as, The Video Vixens, Erotic Heat, and American Strippers on Tour, Erotic Confessions, and Beautiful Kinky Nudes. No other company owns a larger stake in Viewers Choice than Eisner's Mouse House, but the Schweizers said Disney, "won't talk about its role as partner in (Viewer's Choice) or the size of its profits."

More disturbing, the Schweizers say, "The same company that continuously peddles its 'child-friendly' image won't cooperate with police effort to deal with a very real pedophile problem at Disney World.

In fact when informed about Disney The Mouse betrayed, ABC News Prepared a 20/20 segment about it. The News Show had an exclusive contract with the Schweizers, promising that though Disney owned ABC, that fact would not affect the story.

But ABC News cancelled the story, saying only that it, "didn't work."

Ironically, the Eisner autobiography opens with a quote from a Maxwell Anderson, who says, "...inherited morals dissipate as rapidly as inherited wealth." The irony is that Disney may lose both.

Jesus in a colloquy with Peter requested that if he loves him he must: *feed my lambs, tend my sheep, feed my sheep.* (John 21/15-16-17)

Should media be the good shepherd? The Government? The Church? To many, media is Government and Religion.

CHAPTER TEN

DR. LAURA

Laura (Dr. Laura) SCHLESSINGER
America's Straight Shooting Adviser

RIGHTEOUS JEWS BIOS. CONT.

BORN JAN. 1947, BROOKLYN, N.Y. She says that she is a product of an inter-faithless marriage. Her father, born a Jew never mentioned Judaism and her mother, an Italian Catholic, was not serious about religion either. Dr. Laura, her husband and her son made their conversion to Orthodox Judaism in 1988.

She received a B.A. from State Univ. of N.Y., Master's at Columbia, a Post-Doctorial certificate in Marriage, Family and Child Counseling from the University of California. She taught at the Univ. of Malibu, UCLA and Pepperdine and was in private practice for 12years. Her radio show, "Dr. Laura," started in 1990. Her husband, Dr. Lewis Bishop, is her manager and business partner.

Four hundred stations carry her broadcasts. She is admired for her humor and the direct, incisive style that permits her to zero in on a problem. In short, she preaches, teaches, and nags: No sex before marriage, no abortions, no day-care and if possible marry after 30 and stop whining. Take responsibility for your own actions. Homosexuality according to the Bible is an abomination and needs no special status, nor should those so inclined be forced on our children as Scout leaders and teachers.

Of course this courageous stand has made her a lightening-rod for the Homosexual Media-Cabal who are so influential that they could bully major-brand companies to pull their advertising from her radio and TV shows and some markets to have the viewing assigned to the wee hours.

She is the author of best-selling books: *Ten Stupid Things Women Do To Mess Up Their Lives*, and a co-authored with Rabbi Stewart Vogel titled *The Ten Commandment- The significance of God's Laws in Everyday Life*, others: *How could You Do That? – The abdication of Character, Courage and Conscience*, and *Ten Stupid Things Men Do to Mess up Their Lives.*

THE INTERESTS OF CHILDHOOD AND YOUTH ARE
THE INTEREST OF MANKIND.

Janes

CHAPTER ELEVEN

TO ISRAEL

Israel, June 18 To July 10, 1979.
A Back To The Future Adventure

MY WIFE AND I HAD HEARD about a professor from the University of Wisconsin who made yearly journeys to Israel. He'd lead groups mostly from the Alumni of the University of Wisconsin. This would be the sixteenth of his seminars to the "Lands of the Bible, Israel, Greece and Turkey". Before anyone could sign up, the professor, Menahem Mansoor insisted that you attend a weekend preparatory conference in Madison, Wisconsin. It was held on the beautiful campus of an un-filled Catholic Seminary at Benedicts Center, Madison, Wisconsin.

There the professor and Dr. Richard Logon, M.D. and others briefed a group of some thirty-plus attendees on the pending adventure. The weekend was to be a pleasant, but an intense learning time. His zeal and love of the topic was contagious, so much so that groups on these treks became known as "Mansoor's Pilgrim's" or MPs. After we had finished the tour, Menahem or "M.M." once again called everyone to Madison to a banquet to de-brief, savor and exchange anecdotes of our pilgrimage. He didn't give us a test.

JUNE 18/19, 1979

Landed Tel Aviv 7:45 p.m., bussed to Jerusalem by our driver, Shalom Cohen to the Diplomat Hotel. From the window in our room in daylight you could look down on a Bedouin tent, complete with Bedouin family and camel, always ready for "pix-ops" for tourists. Wednesday, June 20-Sholom was waiting in his bus outside the hotel with our guide, Dr. Rivkah Gonew, an archeologist and mother of three. Professor M.M. always saw to our having superior guides and teachers.

The sightseeing took us far south of Jerusalem to what had been before the 1948 War, the division point between Jordan and Israel. Jerusalem along the northern wall of the Old City, atop Mt. Scopes for a panoramic view of the city, where you can see Dome of the Rock, King David Hotel, El Akosor Mosque, Valley of Kidrom, and more. Later we went on Mt. Of Olives where more great sites were. Further sites: buried caves of Johoshaphet, the tomb of the Greek, Roman, Turks and the Crusaders' structures. On to the Western Wall of the Temple Mount where devout Jews, sexes separated by a fence, squeeze messages into the cracks between the stones to commune with God. That evening we attended a concert by the Jerusalem symphony. The program included Schubert, Saint-Saéns, Tchaikovosky, and Prokofiev. Cellist Janos Starker was soloist. One of our pilgrims, Margaret Christy, herself a cellist, renewed her acquaintance with him and with violinist, Wendy Caron, a colleague from the Madison symphony.

THURSDAY, JUNE 21ST

Church of the Holy Sepulcher, the Christian Quarter revealed the tower of the Lutheran Church standing where the Order of the Knights of St. John had a hospital for pilgrims in the time of the Crusades. One of the earliest hospitals in the western world. The church was in bad repair, from an accident in 1927 and an earthquake. It was being reconstructed. We had three clergymen in our group and one read the story of the crucifixion from the Bible. Next to the Dome of the Rock, the site of the Holy of Holies. The Moslems revere it too as the site where Mohammed's horse took him off to Heaven.

Then to Mt. Zion to see the Tomb of King David and nearby the traditional site of the Last Supper and the traditional site of Mary's death, complete with an effigy of Mary asleep.

Now on to Bethlehem and the Church of the Nativity. Originally, it was built by Constantine over a cave where Jesus was born. It has been rebuilt throughout history. In the afternoon we attended a lecture given by M.M. on Judaism.

Friday, June 22ND

Jerusalem, Jericho and Qumran. Our approach to Jericho showed a refreshing green of Date Palms after going through the desert. On the way we passed a near-deserted Refugee Settlement of hundreds of box-like colorless structure, parked in a desert. Not far from there we stopped to look up at the Quarantana Monastery that clings to the sheer side of a mountain. At that time only a few Monks still occupied the Monastery, said to be the site of Christ's temptation. Also, not far was a "tell" of ancient Jericho being excavated. The place has been inhabited since 10,000 B.C., the oldest city in the world. On to the Dead Sea and Qumran, passing several army checkpoints. Qumran was the settlement of the Essenes, the creators of the Dead Sea Scrolls. From the remains of their village just above the level of the Dead Sea you could look at the abrupt backdrop of small mountains and see the entrances to the caves. Some of the caves had held the Scrolls. On the way back to Jerusalem we passed through El-Azariye (Bethany) where Lazarus was raised from the dead.

This afternoon we had two lectures, one of Professor Chairn Rabin, of the Hebrew University on the revival of Hebrew language, and Professor Arye Carman, PhD. From the University of Madison, spoke on Israeli's treatment of immigrants.

Being Friday, we all witnessed the arrival of Shabbat at the Western Wall. I was caught up in a group of young men from a Rabbinical School. At the Western Wall they sang while swaying and dancing, creating a human chain, each with his hand on the shoulder of the man ahead of him. The young man next to me carried a sprig of a live fragrant herb. He shared a piece of the herb with me. It was a brief encounter, but you could sense their joy.

Saturday, June 23ʳᵈ

The Sabbath in Jerusalem, our day for museums. Rockefeller was the first archeological museum in Jerusalem. It had everything from the Neolithic Age skull from Jericho to lintels from the Church of the Holy Sepulcher. Next, the "Shrine of the Book," where the Dead Sea Scrolls are kept. The building is an architectural curiosity, but it is functional. This was followed by the Israeli Museum where there is a wealth of objects of Jewish culture. On leaving, we went to the W.F. Albright Institute of Archeological Research to attend a lecture by Dr. Albert Glock.

Our last call was that evening when we met with Geoffrey and Deborah Wigoder. Deborah was a tall blond Catholic girl when they married years before; Geoffrey, an Irish Jew, who still spoke with a delightful brogue. He is a world scholar, founder of the Museum of the Diaspora in Tel Aviv and has edited and written extensively on religion. We were served punch and cookies as we sat in their cozy garden by a modest dwelling. "Peace" was our topic. At this time, June 1979, it had been about one and a half years (Nov. 1977) since Egyptian President Anwar Sadat's visit to Israel. The peace was tenuous. There were still, "murderous-incidences," of terrorists. Sadat would be assassinated on October 6, 1981. He had received a Nobel Prize for Peace that was shared with Menochem Begin in 1978.

Sunday, June 24ᵀᴴ – More lectures

Monday, June 25ᵀᴴ

Masada! King Herod built and used it about 40 B.C., as refuge from the Jewish people and possibly from Cleopatra of Egypt. Masada was excavated by Yigual Yadin in the early 1960's. It is located atop of a mesa. It is above the Dead Sea, by 440 meters. Because of the dry climate most of the buildings, though roofless, are preserved. Even a dry but usable Mikva was in place. On climbing up, I passed a cavern that had been part of a huge cistern system that had held 40 thousand cubic meters of water that helped sustain the Zealots while besieged by the Romans. Our guide, Dr. Rivkah, gave us a synopsis of the sad story of their deaths, rather than slavery. It was over 100 degrees and you could look down from the fortress and still see the outline in the stones of some of the twelve Roman (Governor) General Silva's Camps.

On the way back to Jerusalem we saw fire and smoke enveloping a vehicle about a quarter mile ahead. The road was winding but not hilly, in an unpopulated area. The vehicle turned out to be a bus and the blaze was awesome as it consumed the bus to a blackened metal skeleton before it was safe for us to pass. We did not know what caused the conflagration, or whether there were injuries, etc. As we passed soldiers and police milled about. Later we were told that the cause was "the bus just overheated."

June 26th

We viewed a model (one to fifty scale) of Jerusalem, as it would have been at the time of the second temple. This was at the site of the Holy Land Hotel. Next, Hadassah Hospital with 12 stained glass windows, designed by Marc Chagall representing the 12 tribes of Israel. From there we went to the Knesset, where we met with Uzzi Baram, a member of the Knesset. He is married to M.M.'s niece. He explained the political parties of Israel. Next, we were met by an old friend of our leader M.M., the Secretary General of the Knesset, Netanel Lorch. He briefed us on the structures and history. We were then guided through the building. In the reception hall, again we found art by Chagall, this time, three tapestries. We ended up there by having lunch among the Knesset members and their functionaries. I recognized a prominent member who later became Prime Minister. In the cafeteria there are separate meat and dairy lines and a stern-faced Rabbi stands guard to make sure there is no breach in the lines.

We then were taken to "Yad Vashem" the Righteous Among the Nations. The Yad Vashem Museum in Israel founded in 1953, honors both Holocaust martyrs and the "Righteous non-Jews" who risked their lives to save the lives of Jews. One could say it is a Holocaust Museum. It is. It can be a sorrowful, draining experience viewing the collection of sad, dreadful pictures and artifacts. Of the countries who had citizens that became rescuers, Poland and the Netherlands were the leaders with the known amount of 5,632 for Poland and 4,464 for the Netherlands. Of the Poles, some 700 of these died while helping their Jewish neighbors. I confess that at the museum I experienced a blush of guilt remembering my long ago silence when I watched at the Boot Camp Barracks, Newport, R.I. some 38 years before, as a group of "Christian" recruits harassed an innocent fellow "Apprentice Seaman," a Jew. They unjustly accused him and degraded him and no one objected. The museum left me limp and tired.

Our next stop was possibly the strangest of all my experiences, though at the time I wasn't aware of it. I believe they named it, "Meditran." It was an inter-cultural community center. It was made up of a small group of dedicated selfless Jews and Arabs working together for a better understanding by their respective societies and of their mutual dependence. Their high idealism may be an answer. I wonder if the group still exists? (Research now shows 30 families still carry on, up from 5 or 6 in 1979.) "Wahat al-salam / Neve Shalom".

We finished the night with a special treat, a Kosher Chinese dinner. The restaurant was at the President Hotel.

WEDNESDAY, JUNE 27TH

Our final day in Jerusalem. That evening we had a banquet honoring our lecturers and guide and officials, which included, Teddy Kollek, the Mayor of Jerusalem and Yegael Yadin, Vice Premier of Israel and a noted archeologist. They both spoke briefly leaving early due to "pressing problems." Yadin disclosed that Israeli planes had been in a dogfight with Syrian jets over

Lebanon and Kollek was having trouble with some of his garbage trucks. The evening was concluded with songs: On Wisconsin, Varsity and "Hatikva" the Israeli national anthem.

THURSDAY, JUNE 28TH

We are now led by a new guide, Avi Shemesh. He is an archeologist and Biblical scholar. We headed for Nazareth; on the way we noted parallel double barbwire fences. Between them a mine field. The path that ran on our side of the fence was made of fine clay and sand, and was swept smooth twice daily. A low-tech, simple method used to disclose the footprints of any infiltrators. It is a border area where the Israeli Kibbutzim have created an agricultural explosion in an otherwise wasteland.

In Nazareth where Jesus spent his childhood, we visited the Church of the Annunciation. It is massive and newer, built in the late 1960s. At a smaller church, St. Joseph, nearby, it was said to have been built over the spot where the Holy Family lived. We descended to a small room above the cave that was the home to Jesus, Mary and Joseph.

Next stop Megiddo. Here is the largest "tell" in Israel. Twenty layers and five sub-layers that it is composed of, dating back to 7,500 B.C. Excavation was begun in 1925. The King Solomon level, about 1,000 B.C. is the most interesting. There you can see his grain silos, stables with stone troughs, the water supply. Our group actually descended the 183 steps to a long damp, cool tunnel leading to the "water." It was dry. Megiddo, where many battles recorded in the Bible were fought, and in some Christian traditions, the final great battle of the World will be fought here at the end of time...Armageddon!

After that we continue on to Mt. Carmel to visit Kamal Mansour the leader of a "Druze" community. He lives in a settlement called, "Issfya." It means windy place. The Druze always live in high places. The Druze people are an anomaly. They are Arab. They number 50,000 in Israel and have existed in the Middle East for a thousand years. They are not Christian, Moslem, or Jewish, but they maintain that they take the best out of all three. Young Druze volunteered to serve in the Israeli armed forces and did serve in the 1948 War and would do so now. Our host Kamal Mansour also ran for the Knesset.

Leaving Carmel Mountain we are headed for Galilee. On the way we pass through Tiberius, then on to Kibbutz, "Nof Ginosar" on the Sea of Galilee, where we will spend two nights. The accommodations included air conditioning, clean, sparse rooms, not unlike our well managed "no frills" motels.

We attended a slide show of the history of this Kibbutz and its government. In a sense, it is a working pure micro-communist society. Of course, it is a commune and in all appearances it was prospering. It is essential that it is peopled by folks who share its philosophies and will carry their load and accept the ground rules: Everyone shares equally regardless of the level of responsibility or work they perform. No one gets paid. Compensation amounts to food, childcare, and clothes. Each couple live in a flat with one bedroom, a living room and a small kitchen for snacks. There is no room for children, or a laundry. The laundry and mending is done centrally. Children live in their own quarters, but dine in a communal dining room with their parents and visit their parents for affection and help with homework. Parents may keep a newborn infant at home for six weeks. After that the baby is cared for by nurses around the clock. For the first year the mother works nearby and can breastfeed her child. By age two they can feed themselves, by twelve they can prepare their own and by thirteen they move from a dorm to their own flats, shared by two girls or two boys with a housemother for 30 children.

I could go on. The Kibbutz movement in Israel had made its contribution. Most are a "success" in both agriculture and in various enterprises, i.e. motels and small manufacturing. They made up approximately 3% of the Israeli population in 1979. I don't know how they now fare.

As the Kibbutz was on the Sea of Galilee, I wanted to say that I had swum there. The water lapped the shore nearby and

I started to wade into it. However, the water barely covered my toes and I was hobbling over "millions" of cobblestone size rocks for at least a quarter of a mile before it reached a depth of about one foot. At this time I am lying prone, my body facing the water and using my hands to pull over the rocks for another quarter of a mile hoping to find total emersion before nightfall. I gave up and made a painful return. It wasn't exactly a "Baptism" but in a way it was.

Before we had left Jerusalem I bought a tennis racquet and balls there and was able to play on the courts by the King David Hotel. The Kibbutz had a court, and I promoted a game with a young man who was a member. Knowing that it would be doubtful of playing again on the trip, I gave the racquet and balls to him. He thanked me profusely, so much so that I perceived that to him, it was a grand present that he alone would own.

Incidentally, the time when I had ventured into the modern part of Jerusalem on my own to buy the tennis racquet and balls, I encountered an Israeli man at a busy corner handing out pamphlets, written in Hebrew. He handed me one and I gave it back saying that I could not read Hebrew. He said "That's alright," and he handed me one in English.

It said, in effect: Please fellow citizen of Israel complain, petition, entreat the government to have us paid weekly or even daily. Now being paid monthly or bimonthly the money loses much of its buying power that it had a week or even a few days before. The pamphlet ended by saying, "Better still have us paid in U.S. dollars."

On returning, Prof. M.M. was visibly upset with me. He said my absence had caused me to miss an important lecture.

FRIDAY, JUNE 29TH

Riding in our bus across the Valley of Ginosar (Gennesaret) to a small church commemorating the miracle of loaves and fishes. On to Capernaum where Jesus began his ministry and on further to the Mount of the Beatitudes where there is a circular church built and maintained by Italian Franciscans.

A service was going on inside and our group gathered on the wide portico that surrounds the church. From there one could look down on the Sea of Galilee. One of the clergy of our group was asked to read the Beatitudes. It was a calm, pleasant day and we were enjoying the serenity, the scent of the flowers, the view, and faint liturgical chants from the inside as our reader went on … "Blessed are the peacemakers; for they shall be called the children…" At that point a squadron of Israeli jets broke the sound barrier with an ear-shattering boom-crack, as they screamed below us, skimming just above the surface of the Sea of Galilee on their way to Lebanon. We understand there was a "dogfight" and the Israelis shot down five Syrian jets. When the jets had passed, our reader continued and read the 8th Psalm, the Lord's Prayer in English and then in Aramaic.

Continuing, the bus took us around the upper part of the Sea of Galilee. We crossed the Jordan River into the Golan Heights, a Syrian stronghold until the 6-Day War in 1967. Sixty Israelis died capturing "Murtafa" there. Before that, Syria had commanded the whole area. On the way back to Kibbutz Nof Ginosar, our bus picked up a few hitchhiking soldiers in full field military uniforms, including automatic rifles. On seeing them, I realized how I might have been viewed so very young in the service during WWII. We finished the evening with Sabbath dinner, folk singing and dancing.

Saturday, June 30th

Galilee to Tel Aviv by way of Akko and Haifa. In Akko we toured the Crusader Citadel and even used the narrow dank escape tunnel, noted graffito on the walls, left by homesick Crusaders. On to Haifa, where we went directly to the Bahai Temple. I thought it odd to have a major temple in a land of Jews and Moslems. Back near our home in Glenview, Illinois, in the village of Wilmette, there is an architectural gem of one of the Bahai Temples. It is an attraction. The one in Haifa, too, was special, but the grounds and landscaping would be worthy of an architectural jewel. We were guided about by a man and wife team, Mr. and Mrs. Gibson. Our next destination, Tel Aviv, the luxurious Diplomat Hotel, right on the beach. It almost seemed like we were back in the U.S. except for armed soldiers strapped with sub-machine guns guarding every entrance. Even so, a holiday spirit was in the air. The hotel backed to the ocean water. Lots of soft sand and volleyball, beach umbrellas and families enjoying the sun could be seen.

SUNDAY JULY 1ST

We rose early and bussed to Caesarea, the Roman capital of Palestine for 500 years. It is just north of Tel Aviv. We were met by Professor Robert Bull, archeologist from Indiana University. He guided us on a tour of excavations he was overseeing. We saw the aqueduct, the second century Hippodrome, Crusader Fortress, and public buildings; one he felt was the library. At a non-descript, rather plain field, Prof. Bull brushed away sand and earth and uncovered a mosaic with a Greek inscription from the Bible: Romans 13, verses 1-7, and then covered it again. He told us of the enormity of his task, the archaeological treasures right under your feet, "there's several lifetimes of work here," and he only had a handful of college students for his help and only for part of the year.

Back to Tel Aviv we visited the Museum of the Diaspora. Our friend, Geoffrey Wigoder, with whom we had refreshments in his garden back on June 23rd, is a founder of the Museum, and he took time to guide us this day. After going through it, I felt that had I spent a couple of days instead of an hour, I could have qualified for a Master's degree in Jewish history. It is not a true museum but devotes everything shown to telling the story of the 1900+ years' history of the dispersion of the Jewish people from the Holy land.

The Israeli portion of our adventure was over.

JULY 2ND TO JULY 10TH

From there we went to Athens, Greece, then boarded the cruise ship "Oceanus", made stops at Rhodes, Crete, Patmos,

Mykonos, Ephesiss and in Istanbul, Turkey. The ship's captain gave our group a cocktail party in celebration of our 4th of July, and we "Pilgrims" improvised a skit that put historic figures from our Revolution and Civil Wars to joining us as fellow "Pilgrims." This last portion was enriching but I wanted to relate the Israeli experience primarily. The tour was profound, yet troubling.

There have been promises of peace but this historic sliver of real estate called Israel, not as big as the state of Delaware (and getting smaller), has been the fuse that ignites terrorist acts there and all over the planet. The United States is perceived as not just a friend of Israel, but the engine that drives it.

The heroic efforts by Anwar Sadat and later by Israel's Prime Minister Yetzhat Yadin resulted in their assassination at the hands of their own nationals.

No Islamic state wants a direct confrontation with the U.S. The answer is "stealth." War without a country attached to it, a war of terror against everyone, civilians, women, children, armed forces, businesses, infrastructures, utilities, health facilities and more, lots of targets.

Both the Islamics and Israelis have moderates in their camps that would accommodate a "live and let live" situation. However, pragmatists are hard to find anymore because they tend to get assassinated.

Jesus was asked by the Pharisees, "When the kingdom of God would come..." and he answered saying, that it doesn't come with observation, nor will it be here or there ... but he said, "For indeed the kingdom of God is within you."

Certainly on a natural plane the Jews have amply demonstrated the gifts that God has put within them. A physical "homeland" is a redundancy. So saying does not solve the problem. Neither does the constant killing and retaliations and, of course, having our country caught in the crossfire.

There are things that ought to be initiated. Because the terror is fed by money from energy, let's become energy-independent, even an energy exporter. With reasonable ecologic safe guards let's open up, unlock our vast wealth in energy resources. We have huge oil potentials beneath our public lands. Is there any reason that our government shouldn't receive the handsome royalties that the Saudis & the Emirates are getting? We also have massive amounts of energy locked in shale deposits. These deposits exceed all the oil in the Middle East, and they can be extracted cleanly and safely. Of course, we should accelerate our work on fuel cells, hydrogen, fusion, fission, wind and water power too, but we have under foot enough raw energy to carry us for the next two centuries.

Take the incentives, the money away, or reduce it through real competition, and they'll fold their terrorist tents and join the world of capitalists. For defense, refineries should be built at the most productive well-heads of government tracts. Pipe lines for joint private and government use can be installed. This too would go a long way toward easing to balance of trade deficit and lower our manufacturing costs.

Also, there is another front that can be opened in concert with the aforesaid, and goes along with the theme of this book. Let's have our super media organs adopt the ethnic faces of the region and begin to produce audio visuals that speak their language. Our entertainment industry is already international. Let's clean it up. It now sells decadence, depravity or pablum. It can be offensive to Moslems and many Americans. Nonetheless, it is so pervasive and powerful that it constantly is capable of shaping and bending opinions. Have a "Manhattan Project" to put a shiny new face on Israel and the United States." "Let us entertain them." Show our commonality, the qualities of usefulness to mankind. Note some of the Righteous Jews and the righteous among all our people. Tell, it, tell it, tell it!! (*I am indebted to journals kept by my wife & self and fellow MPs, Laura and Joyce Bartell for the Israeli recollections.*)

CHAPTER TWELVE

HYMAN RICKOVER

Hyman George Rickover Father of Nuclear Navy

Admiral Hyman Rickover

THE COLD WAR COULD NOT have been won had not the US achieved awesome submarine preeminence. The protean versatile atomic submarines assured that the balance of power was always tilted to the US benefit. It was because of Rickover persistence that the Navy built the first atomic-powered sub.

He was born in Russia in 1900 to Rachel and Abraham Rickover. His father, a tailor, had immigrated to the US and lived in Chicago. Hyman on graduation from high school received an appointment to the United States Naval Academy, where he was commissioned an ensign. He did graduate work in electrical engineering. In 1929 he received an MS degree from Columbia University.

He had many assignments at sea and ashore. At the start of WW-2 he was put in charge of electrical section of the Bureau of Ships in Washington. In 1946 he was assigned to Oakridge, the site of the atomic bomb development. He became convinced that the navy should begin to make a nuclear submarine, though he was at that time alone in that belief. However, by 1947 he prevailed and headed the project. Components came in from many centers, especially Idaho and Groton CT. In 1954 the first atomic powered submarine, The Nautilus was launched.

Rickover was controversial, due to out-spoken opinions and unorthodox methods causing him to be twice passed over for promotion, but later, through the intervention of congressional leaders, he was promoted: Rear Admiral (1953), Vice Admiral (1958), and Admiral (1973). He retired in 1982 and died in 1986. A friend of mine, Gordon McClarren, a graduate of the Naval Academy and an atomic specialist, had trained on a cruise on the Nautilus and served on its successor. When he presented his credentials to Admiral Rickover, the Admiral noted that my friend was a good scholar but, that besides science, he should have taken more of the classic literature.

He was critical of the US education system. One of the books he has written in 1963, *"American Education; A National Failure,"* should be read.

COWARDICE ASKS, IS IT SAFE? EXPEDIENCY ASKS, IS IT POLITIC? VANITY ASKS, IS IT POPULAR? BUT CONSCIENCE ASKS, IS IT RIGHT?

Punshon

Righteous Jews bios to follow

CHAPTER THIRTEEN

THE SHIP JEROBOAM

HERE AGAIN MELVILLE PROVIDES a "mad" prophet. This time a crewman, not a mate nor a harpooner, but a fellow who started as a lowly deck hand who has deluded the Jeroboam's crew into believing he was the reincarnation of the angel Gabriel.

He had real acting skill and the cunning of a street-magician in achieving control of the simple seamen. Because of this the captain could not discipline nor censor him without incurring their enmity in an already troubled ship. He was given the freedom to pick and choose to work or not. It was "Gabriel" who deemed to join in crewing a boat from the Jeroboam to the Pequod for "kind of Gam." Captain Mayhem declined boarding the Perquod because his ship was experiencing an epidemic, instead exchanged news with Ahab from his boat. He relates how his first mate, Macy, was recently killed by Moby Dick. At this point "Gabriel" shouts to Ahab that he will follow Macy because Moby Dick is a divinity. Ironically Ahab has a letter for Macy from his wife but "Gabriel" thwarts its delivery by prematurely giving the signal to row back.

The prophets in the story; Melville portrays them as mystic-gadflies. Might they represent today's concerned folks that see doom and disaster for our culture under the new Ahabs? Melville Prophets and Starbuck (a creature of the Establishment) are concerned, but they can't stop the coming calamity in the novel.

CHAPTER FOURTEEN

"PIP"

———

PIPPIN, CALLED PIP, IS THE little cheerful black lad who readily assists all of "ship's company," carrying water, gear, etc., always to a bouncy cadence and the rhythm of his tambourine. Because he is not robust he is assigned as a "ship's-keeper," to stay on board, while stronger hands man the whaleboats during a whale chase.

When one of Stub's men sprains his hand, he takes a chance putting Pip in his place. It is a mistake. Pip, on seeing a whale in close, twice jumps out of the boat into the ocean. The second time Pip is lost as the whale pulls the boat out of site leaving poor Pip lost in the immensity of the great ocean. Eventually, but just by chance, he is found and rescued. However, the experience unhinges him and from then on he is no longer coherent nor responsive. He is now considered an idiot and goes about blathering and banging on his tambourine to invisible audiences.

Strangely, Ahab relates to his madness and is drawn to him. He has him live in his cabin, but does nothing for him towards restoring his faculties. Pip remains dependant.

This opens the deafening silence of Media regarding the masses of blacks, Hispanics and others attending Public Schools that after 10 or 12 years can barely read or do math but they will be patronized, subsidized, succored, hospitalized and many times incarcerated much of their lives at the tax paying citizen's expense to keep them and the big Teacher's Unions content.

Ahab, of course, is insane. What excuse can Media, teacher's Unions, (and their surrogates, the various limp legislative bodies) have?

CHAPTER FIFTEEN

THE ENDANGERED SPECIES

THE WRITER HAS ISHMAEL show great respect for the whales and intones fear of their extinction when he says, "...the moot point is whether the Leviathan can long endure so wide a chase...at last be exterminated...and the last whale, like the last man, smoke his pipe and evaporate in the last puff...comparing the humped herd of whales with the humped herds of buffalo (American Bison circa 1851), which not 40 years ago, overspread by tens of thousands the prairies of Illinois and Missouri and shook their iron manes...thunder clotted brows upon sites...where now polite brokers sell you land. In such a comparison an irresistible argument would seem furnished to show...that the whale cannot escape speedy extinction."

Unfortunately, he continues and completely rationalizes away that position, saying that the oceans are so large and the whales have so many places inaccessible to man that their numbers can not be exhausted by even an armada of ships and the puny men in little boats throwing harpoons at them. He sums it up by saying, "In as much as the Leviathan comes floundering down upon us from the headwaters of eternities... they are destined to be around."

He could not foresee the huge diesel-operated factory ships that cannon-launch harpoon missiles that explode after penetrating the whale's body. Ships made with special inclined opened sterns equipped with hoists so efficient and quick that even the sharks are cheated of their free lunch.

Media seem to share the philosophy that, "...Humanity has come floundering down from the eternities and will always be malleable and inexhaustible," and TV has given them The Factory Ships.

Humanity is fragile and not inexhaustible but it has a resilience and strength from an unaccounted source. The Pequad's frame is yet frailer.

CHAPTER SIXTEEN

THE GEEK SHOW

THE OLD TRAVELING CARNIVALS and smaller circuses had, besides the Ferris wheel, Merry-Go-Round, thrill-rides, try-your-skill games, etc. the Side Shows, which included The Freak Show. A premium of that would be The Geek Show. It was never called that. "Geek," was an inside name. It was the name that "Carnies," gave to an individual who had sunk to a sub-human level and would do anything to satisfy the drug and/or alcohol need. For his "fix" and keep, he'd perform as "The Wild man brought up by animals. He doesn't speak any known human language, etc." The elected derelict addict would "perform" in an animal cage wearing a dog's collar and chains. His act many times included biting off the head of a live chicken; tear it apart and feign devouring it amongst feathers and blood. Today the word "Geek" has come to have a synonymous meaning as "nerd" or an excessively driven computer devotee; far from the old meaning.

To the old Carnies and small Circuses, The Geek Show was profitable because they knew viewing shocking, outrageous degradation of a human level had an appeal for the bumpkins and the dim wits.

Today many TV stations feature updated versions of the Geek Shows. Two come to mind; The Jerry Springer and The Howard Stern Show. These two, ugh! "...Showmen," would make the Komodo dragon, a ten foot long, 300lb., bad breathed, man eating lizard a house pet, to go along with their shows' guests. Both have dug under rocks to find the most dysfunctional, perverse sad dregs and Porn-Queens to titillate their viewers, the 49.5 IQ crowd. Of course their sponsors are anxious to exploit this "market."

Howard Stern's degenerate drivel on the Columbine massacre: *"There were some really good-looking girls running out with their hands over their heads. "Did those kids (the suspects) try to have sex with any of the good-looking girls? They didn't even do that? At least if you're going to kill yourself and kill all the kids, why wouldn't you have sex? If I was going to kill some people, I'd take them out with sex."*

Incidentally, Seagram Inc. owns The Jerry Springer Show and the Record Co. that distribute Marilyn Manson music.

The above, though driven by moral-less, entities, has the primary aim of making money. The following has achieved that goal in spades and at the same time can claim that it has wrought profound social changes albeit changes dear to the developer's heart. I'm talking about:

CHAPTER SEVENTEEN

ALL IN THE FAMILY

HISTORY WILL RECORD THIS SERIES as the most potent social/
political video "cartoons" ever made. Norman Lear's creation
may never be surpassed. New expressions were put into the
American Lexicon. It was and is the most entertaining way to be
brainwashed. Of course the fortunate pick of actors helped too.
It featured the late Carol O'Connor as Archie, the lovable bigot.
The show's first telecast on CBS was in January 1971, and the last
episode in April 1979. Yet today it is still being widely broadcast
carrying its series of "messages."

I wouldn't dare utter a conservative sentence in front of one
of my daughters for fear of being tagged, (or re-tagged) as a,
"walking, talking, living, breathing Archie Bunker." Other folks
of my persuasion have to be on guard lest they too are so labeled.

Certainly Archie's bumbling and his malapropism makes the
"medicine" go down easier. He could be the "in front," buffoon
for holding blatant politically incorrect ideas innocently because
"we" know he hasn't had the advantage of an enlightened
education.

The show explored a wide gamut of situations that a family
may encounter and was always able to lampoon an "incorrect
attitude" with humor.

CHAPTER EIGHTEEN

A CLOSE TO HOME STORY

WHEN I WAS 8 GOING ON 9 years old the great movie, "Tarzan, The Ape Man," with Johnny Weissmuller, made every American boy a Tarzan.

I could make a yell, I'd swear, sounded just like Tarzan's. One day when I was playing with a group of boys about my age, we set out to climb some trees in a small woods in the Oak Lane section of Philadelphia. I commandeered my own special tree and climbed out on a stout limb, and gave the Tarzan yell, arms extended, sprang to and grabbed another limb from which I intended to swing and reach a heavier branch (just like Tarzan). Unfortunately the limb was rotted and dead and I dropped 30+ feet into a creek bed that was only inches deep.

My head was gashed and bleeding. My companions abandoned their trees and came to my aid and assisted me out to the nearest street, "Old York Road." It must have been a Saturday. There was little traffic on this normally busy street, no cars, no trolleys. Shortly a truck belonging to our neighborhood green-grocer (The City Line Market) stopped. The driver knew us and our families. I was lifted into the back of the canvas covered truck and was accompanied by two or three of the boys on a rapid drive to the Jewish Hospital (now named The Albert Einstein Medical Center) about 4 or 5 miles away. I remember leaning on one of my friends and noting that his shirt turned crimson from my bleeding.

There is a happy ending to the story. I've lived to an old age, had other adventures and close calls. The reason I relate this happening is to show how very impressionable the young can be. How even a wholesome stimulus such as a Tarzan movie of 1932 could have ended in a serious injury or even death. To an 8 year old I was really about to be Tarzan.

Media has responsibility. Today there are stories of kids being maimed and dying when they emulate or imitate stunts seen on TV and movies, trying to do what is "suggested."

Besides pornography, the most pernicious modes of suggestion are the, "Video Games." Here Virtual Reality becomes reality with some individuals who become so mesmerized by the "games" that they recede to a form of sleepwalk (somnambulate) to a post hypnotic state where they scheme to fulfill the roles they've practiced (rehearsed) playing the game time after time. It has been said that the perpetrators of the Columbine Massacre and other similar tragedies were Video Game addicts. I have watched individuals hone their skills and reflexes at killing the "Bad Guys" at their own VCR, etc. sets. In the case of Columbine one might say that the psychic chemistry may have already existed due to heredity and/or environment, etc., but the (audio-visual) Video Games provided the ignition cap that brought about the explosions.

Certainly Pornography has triggered rapes, murders and vile disgusting behavior. Our species survives by imitation. Imitation is a builtin learning tool, but it is easily perverted, especially when media graphically licenses the diversion. I have mused many times as I've viewed a Chinese figurine of three monkeys: one covering its eyes, another its ears and the last its mouth. "See no evil, Hear no evil and Speak no evil." The Ancient Chinese saw wisdom in shunning evils. Contrast that with the way our media diagrams methods of seeing, hearing and talking, the foolish, the harmful, the evil. The authors of our Bill of Rights did not foresee nor intend that the First Amendment would be used to shelter pornographers, bomb making terrorists and maniacs. It was created as a safeguard for the arena of ideas and political differences for the good of all the people. Porn and violence degrades humanity to levels below that of the animals.

Talk about the influence of cinema on people: as a boy I wanted to be Tarzan, but after my tree accident I was inclined to look for other qualities besides swinging from tree to tree or swimming faster than a crocodile. I had discovered Will Rogers, his easy "down-home" ad-lib talks on his radio show (I believe sponsored by Gulf Oil) and his movies. Every Saturday my folks gave me 16 cents to see a movie; 10 cents to get in plus 1 cent "entertainment tax" and a nickel to buy a box of "Good and Plenty" candy.

The nearest theatre was called the Erlin, about two miles away, but right on City Line Rd. on the Philly side. Our house was a stone's throw from City Line. Walking was the only option. Saturday at a movie was an adventure. First came the serial cliffhanger – maybe Flash Gordon, next a short feature, sometimes Laurel and Hardy, and finally the feature – like "A Yankee in King Arthur's Court," starring Will Rogers. Of course, there were other pictures that didn't have Will Rogers, but I made it a point to see his even if it meant a trolley ride to another neighborhood. I took great delight in the Will Rogers movies because I felt I knew him personally because he'd "talk to me" on another medium, radio every week.

Shortly after my eleventh birthday, my dad died. He was 48 years old, a smoker and the greatest man in the world. That was November, 1934.

Part of the summer (1935) was spent at the Germantown Boys Club "camp" in Ocean City, N.J. One day after playing in the surf, jumping each incoming wave again and again, I retreated to the hot sandy beach and headed for the cool sand under the boardwalk. On the way, I was passing a man and woman beside their beach umbrella. I overheard them saying that they had just been told that Will Rogers was killed in an airplane crash in Alaska.

It seemed as though I had lost my father again. I couldn't articulate my grief, but a sad pall drew over the rest of my stay. The only consolation I drew was that I was not alone, that much of the nation grieved too.

Does anyone in that business realize the extent of how massive their influence can be? How powerful, how useful, or how destructive? I wish they knew.

Disseminating and glamorizing criminal, erotic, dysfunctional life-styles through the mass media cause criminal behavior in some. There is no such thing as a victimless crime. However broadcasting and exalting cleanliness and virtue can deter crimes.

CHAPTER NINETEEN

JEWS IN THE PERFORMING ARTS

The following is a list of Jewish entertainers from the disciplines, of the past and the present. (With today's recording technology many times they merge). It is not complete but it shows the preponderance of superb Jewish talents that are part and parcel to media exposure. With several blatant exceptions, most do not espouse the life-style promoted by the media: movies, TV sitcoms, etc.

Maurice Abravanel
Aaron Avsholomov
Mario Ancona
Joseph Achron
Lauren Bacall
Willi Apel
Guido Adler
Abraham Baer
Alan Arkin
Sarah Adler
Daniel Barenboin
Beatrice Arthur
Emanuel A. Aguelar
Gene Barry
Vladimir Ashkenazy
Martin Allen
Paul Bekker
Leopold Auer
Milton Berle

Morey Amsterdam
Isidor Achron
Victor Babin
George Antheil
Joey Adams
Burt Bacharach
Louis Applebaum
Larry Adler
Martin Balsam
Harold Arlen
Theodor Adorno
John Barnett
Misha Asheroff
Charles Alkan
Jeff Barry
Ed Asner
Woody Allen
Jack Benny
Morris Carnovsky

Peter Falk

Jack Carter

Gertrude Berg

Harvey Fierstein

Jill Clayburgh

Sarah Bernhardt

Eddie Fisher

Myron Cohen

Leonard Bernstein

Leon Fleisher

Norm Crosby

Abraham Binder

Phil Foster

Tony Curtis

Joey Bishop

Allen Funt

Mario Castelnuovo

Andra Bloch

John Garfield

Federico Consolo

Felix Blumenfield

Uri Gellar

Lili Darvas

Arthur Bodanzky

Estelle Getty

Neil Diamond

Tom Bosley

Jack Gilford

Ludwig Donath

David Brenner

Philip Glass

Kirk Douglas

Elkie Brooks

Benny Goodman

Mel Brooks

Irving Berlin

Totie Fields

Jeff Chandler

Shelley Berman

Avery Fisher

Lee J. Cobb

Elmer Bernstein

Bud Flanagan

Irwin Corey

Theodore Bikel

Lukas Foss

Billy Crystal

Eduard Birbaum

David Frye

Aaron Copland

Mel Blanc

Martin Gabel

Edouard Colonne

Clair Bloom

Art Garfunkel

Rodney Dangerfield

Jerry Bock

George Gerschwin

Howard DaSilva

Victor Borge

Stan Getz

Misha Dicter

Lucienne Bre'val

Hermoine Gingold

Antal Dorati

Fanny Brice

Alma Gluck

Richard Dreyfuss

Phil Silver

Paul Dukas

Ernest Gold
Jacqueline du Pre'
Lenny Bruce
Elliott Gould
Ramblin Jack Elliott
Ignaz Brull
Eydie Gorme
Herb Edelman
George Burns
Lee Grant
Joel Engel
Sid Caesar
Noah Greenberg
Camille Erlanger
Eddie Canter
Joel Grey
Morton Feldman
Hugo Hiss
Tony Martin
Andre Koselanetz
Judy Holiday
Elaine May
Bert Lahr
Vladimir Horowitz
Yehudi Menuhin
Steve Lawrence
Leslie Howard
Giacomo Meyerbeer
Pinky Lee
Marty Ingles
Mich Miller
Loyya Lenya
Carl Jaffe
Pier Monteux
Sam Levenson

Joyce Brothers
Boris Goldovsky
Bob Dylan
John Browning
Morton Gould
Vivian Ellis
Manfred Bukofzer
Virginia Graham
Misch Elman
Red Buttons
Lorne Green
Alvin Epstein
Dyan Cannon
Shecky Greene
David Ewen
Kitty Carlisle
Arlo Guthrie
Erich Korngold
Duston Hoffman
Jackie Mason
Serge Koussevizky
Oscar Homilka
Felix Mendelssohn
Ruth Laredo
Harry Houdini
Robert Merrill
Evelyn Lear
Janis Ian
Darius Milhaud
Erich Leinsdorf
Lou Jacobi
Nathan Milstein
Jack E. Leonard
Harry James
Zero Mostel

Sid James   Sam Levine
Jan Murry   George Jessel
Jerry Lewis   Bess Myerson
Billy Joel   Shari Lewis
Isaac Nathan   Al Jolson
Ted Lewis   Julia Neilson
Emile Jonas   Oscar Levant
Alfred Newman   Rafael Joseffy
Raymond Lewenthal   Phyllis Newman
Madeline Kahn   Hal Linder
Mike Nichols   Milt Kamen
Max Linder   Jacques Offenbach
Marv Kaplan   Philip Loeb
David Oistrakh   Danny Kaye
Frank Loesser   Igor Oistrakh
Stubby Kaye   Frederick Loewe
Eugene Ormandy   Louis Kentner
George London   Lili Palmer
Harvey Keitel   Perter Lorre
Jan Pierce   Jerome Kern
Paul Lukas   Itzhak Pearlman
Alan King   Gustav Mahler
Murry Perahia   Carol King
Barry Manilow   Roberta Peters
Alexander Kipnis   Marcel Marceau
Gregor Piatigorsky   Igor Kipnis
Hal March   Otto Preminger
Leon Kirchner   Marx Brothers
Andre Previn   Otto Klemperer
Walter Matthau   Louise Rainer
Jack Klugman   Bette Milder
Tony Randall   Leonid Kogan
Janet Margolin   Carl Reiner
Harvey Korman   Ross Martin
Don Rickles   Ritz Brothers

Rod Seiger
Edward G. Robinson
George Solti
Isaac Stern
Richard Rogers
Arnold Stang
Larry Storch
Leonard Rose
Howard Stern
Barbara Streisand
Susan Strasberg
Jule Styne
David Susskind
Geo. Szell
Henry Szeryng
Joseph Szigeti
Michael Tilson Thomas
Three Stooges
Richard Tucker
Erich von Stroheim
Alfred Wallenstein
Eli Wallach
Bruno Walter
David Warfield
Leonard Warren
Paul Whiteman
Gene Wilder
Henry Winkler
Shelley Winters
Ed Wynn
Henry Youngman
Pinchas Zukerman

Joseph Silverstein
Wm. Steinberg
Maxie Rosenbloom
Stephen Sonheim
Rise Stevens
Artur Rodzinsky
Jerry Springer
Oscar Straus
Lillian Roth
Anton Rubinstein
Arthur Rubinstein
Mort Sahl
Soupy Sales
Jill St. John
Kurt Sanderling
Jose Schildkrout
Artur Schnabel
Alexander Schneider
Arnold Schoenberg
Gunther Schuller
Wm. Schuman
George Segal
Peter Sellers
Rudolf Serkin
Wm. Shatner
Artie Shaw
Dick Shawn
Norma Shearer
Allan Sherman
Dinah Shore
Silvia Sidney
Beverly Sills

Righteous Jews Continued

CHAPTER TWENTY

JUDY RESNICK

American Astronaut

BORN APRIL 1949...Died January 29, 1986 Judith was on the ill-fated shuttle, Challenger, when it exploded.

Her grandparents emigrated from the Ukraine in 1924 to Palestine and in 1929 came to the US with their son Marvin, Judith's father. She was born in Ohio and brought up in Akron. In high school she

Judith Resnick, Astronaut

was a member of the Honor Society, The French Club and The Math Club. She had a perfect score on the Scholastic Aptitude and Math Tests. She also studied and played classical piano, received an Electrical Engineering Degree from Carnegie-Mellon University, and a Doctorate from the University of Maryland.

Before becoming an Astronaut she had worked for Xerox Corp., R.C.A. Corp. and The National Institute of Health.

In 1984 she served as a Mission Specialist aboard Discovery performing solar power experiments and other complex tasks.

She had spent about 145 hours in space before the Challenger tragedy.

Her father Dr. Marvin Resnick said, (in effect) "Despite what happened...I know Judith would feel that The Space Program should continue..."

LIFE IS EITHER A DARING ADVENTURE OR NOTHING. TO KEEP OUR FACES TOWARDS CHANGE AND BEHAVE LIKE FREE SPIRITS IN THE PRESENCE OF FATE IS STRENGTH UNDEFEATABLE.

Helen Keller

CHAPTER TWENTY-ONE

YEHUDE MENUHIM

Extraordinary Violinist and Human Being

Born in 1916 in N.Y. City...Died in 1999 in Europe.

His parents, Moshe and Marutha were born in Russia. The Menuhim family trace their decent from a long line of Hasidic rabbis.

Yehude started serious violin lessons at age 5 and by age 7or 8 gave a performance with the San Francisco Symphony. He was also a product of Home-Schooling where he became proficient in Math, History, Hebrew, French, German, Italian, and Spanish. At age 10 the family traveled to Europe. While in Paris he studied with framed composer, violinist Georges Enesco.

In 1927 at age 11 or 12 he played to an overflow crowd at Carnegie Hall. His sister, Hephzibah was an accomplished pianist and sometimes they played together. In 1934 he went on his first World Tour and performed 110 engagements in 13 countries. At the finish of the tour at age 19 he took 2 years off for self-examination. It may have been during this time at the family estate near Los Gatos, California that he became interested in Yoga and Homeopathy.

In 1937 he resumed performing. The rest of his career is history. During WW2 he gave hundreds of concerts, many to our troops over seas. At the end of the war he performed both as a violinist and conductor.

He founded Switzerland's Gstaad Festival, was music director of England's Bath Festival. He founded two schools for music students, wrote several books, received honorary British Knighthood and awards from France, Germany, Belgium and Greece.

He was a well informed layman in the medical discipline known as Homeopathy. He wrote the Foreword of a book by Dr. Barry Rose, *The Family Guide to Homeopathy*. In part he says, "...As a musician, what I particularly love about it is the great effect of subtlety-the enormous response to an infinitesimal but crucial intervention.

IMPARTING KNOWLEDGE IS ONLY LIGHTING OTHER MEN'S CANDLE AT OUR LAMP WITHOUT DEPRIVING OURSELVES OF ANY FLAME.

Jane Porter

CHAPTER TWENTY-TWO

GERTRUDE B. ELION

1988 Nobel Prize Winner

Gertrude B. Elion

BORN IN N.Y. CITY IN 1918.

Her father Robert, at age 12, emigrated from Lithuania. Her mother Bertha Cohen arrived from Russia by herself at age 14. Years later, after they had met and married, they brought love of music and education as an integral part of their union. Because of the depression, for Gertrude or "Trudy" the chances of going to college were slim. Fortunately her grades in school were so high that she won admission to Hunter College with no tuition charge. She graduated Phi Beta Kappa.

She attended graduate school while working as a doctor's receptionist and a substitute teacher in N.Y. City High Schools until 1942. WW2 had begun, creating a shortage of male chemists. This led to her working at the American Headquarters of the British pharmaceutical firm, Burroughs Wellcome in Tuckahoe, N.Y.

At Burroughs Wellcome she collaborated with Georgia Hitchings on drugs that could interrupt the life cycle of abnormal cells, leaving healthy ones untouched. This led to an 80% survival rate for childhood leukemia. Before this development it was virtually 100% fatal. The research also helped prevent kidney transplant rejection and aided in treatment of hepatitis, severe rheumatoid arthritis and auto-immune lupus. When George Hitchings retired she became head of the department and helped bring about drugs that combat shingles, genital herpes, chicken-pox, and herpes encephalitis.

Thrilled at being a Nobel Prize recipient, she said, "It's very nice, but that not what's its all about." She also received the National Medal of Science.

THE TRUE TEST OF CIVILIZATION IS NOT THE CENSUS, NOR THE SIZE OF CITIES, NOR THE CROPS, BUT THE KIND OF MAN (PERSON) THAT THE COUNTRY TURNS OUT.

Emerson

Righteous Jews will follow

CHAPTER TWENTY-THREE

SLAVERY

Prof. Walter Williams

SLAVERY SURVIVES AND THRIVES in Africa (from Washington Times January 15-21 2001) – by Walter Williams

Black slaves are still available – just not in the United States. To make a purchase you would have to travel to the Sudan as Gerald Williams, Harvard University pre-med student, did in October 2000. Slavery in the Sudan is in part a result of a 15-year war by the Muslim north against the black Christian and Animist south. Arab militias, armed by the Khartoum government, raid villages, mostly those of the Dinka tribe. They shoot the men and enslave the women and children. Women and children are kept as personal property or they're taken north and auctioned off.

In Sudanese slave markets, a woman or child can be purchased for $90. An Anti-Slavery International investigator interviewed Abuk Akwar. A 13-year-old girl who, along with 24 other children, was captured by the militia, marched north and given to a farmer. The investigator reported, "throughout the day she worked in his sorghum *fields and at night in his bed. During the march she was raped and called a black donkey." The girl managed to escape with the help of the master's jealous wife.*

Mr. Williams visited the Sudan as part of an eight person delegation sponsored by Christian Solidarity International (CSI). CSI, as well as the Boston-based American Anti-Slavery Group (AASG), have a stopgap mission of buying, at a cost of $85 each, Christian African women and children whom Muslims capture and enslave. AASG's purchase emancipates them.

Mr. Williams' tales of Muslim atrocities are horrific. Six-year-old Mawien Ahir Bol failed to clean a goat pen to his master's satisfaction. The penalty: his index finger was cut off. Yak Kenyang Adieu's punishment for being too sick to mind his master's goats was the loss of all fingers on his right hand. Mr. Williams' trip freed, through purchase, these two boys and 20 other slaves. Should you be interested in learning more about slavery, the American Anti-Slavery Group's website is: *www.anti-slavery.com.*

Chattel slavery also exists in the former French colony of Mauritania, where it was officially outlawed in 1980. The U.S. State department estimated that as of 1994 there were 90,000 blacks living as property of Berbers. The Berbers use their slaves for labor, sex and breeding. They are also exchanged for camels, trucks, guns or money. Slave offspring becomes the property of the master. According to a 1990 Human Rights Watch report, routine Mauritanian slave punishments include beating, denial of food and prolonged exposure to the sun, with hands and feet tied together. Serious infringements of the master's rule can mean prolonged horrible tortures such as the "insect treatment"-where the slave is bound head and foot and insects placed in her ears and other body orifices- and "burning coals," where the slave is bound and buried with hot coals placed on parts of his body.

The American Anti-Slavery Group says, "most distressing is the silence of the American media whose reports counted for so much in the battle to end Apartheid in South Africa." Only recently and thankfully so, have mainstream black organizations such as the Congressional Black Caucus and the National Association for the Advancement for Colored People taken a stand against chattel slavery in Mauritania and Sudan. At *one time Minister Louis Farkhan simply denied that his brother Muslims could perpetrate such an injustice, but now has he quietly accepted the evidence. Jesse Jackson remains silent.*

Slavery is not the only injustice that goes practically ignored. There are the frequent outbreaks of genocide in Rwanda, Burundi, Liberia and the Congo. In fact, it is fairly safe to say that most of today's most flagrant human rights abuses occur in Africa. But unfortunately they get little attention-maybe it's because Africans instead of Europeans are the perpetrators. Europeans are held accountable to civilized standards of behavior, while African's aren't.

EXCEPT FOR OCCASIONAL SUNDAY SUPPLEMENTS AND A CONSERVATION PAPER, THE ABOVE COULD GO ON AND ON AND VERY FEW WOULD EVER KNOW.

Righteous Jews Continued

CHAPTER TWENTY-FOUR

IRVING BERLIN

America's Beloved Song Poet

ANOTHER GIFT FROM THE OLD WORLD, he was born in Russia (Siberia) 1888 and died in 1989 living over 101 years. One of eight children to Moses and Leah Baline. Moses was a Canter.

When Irving was eight years old and in the 2nd grade, to help his family, he quit school and sold newspapers. As a teenager he was a singing

Irving Berlin

waiter. He had no musical training, self taught to play the piano but only using the black keys. By a printing error on the cover of his first composition it gave the composer's name as, "I. Berlin" instead of Baline. He kept it for the rest of his life. His first song was "Marie from Sunny Italy." He earned less than a dollar for it. His number 1 great success came in 1911 with "Alexander's Ragtime Band."

In 1913 he married Dorothy Goetz. While on their Honeymoon in Cuba she contracted typhoid and died. He wrote a love song, "When I Lost You," in her memory. It wasn't until 1926 that he married again, this time to the daughter of a wealthy Catholic business tycoon. It was big news at the time. They had three daughters.

In 1917 he was drafted into the Army as a private. During this time he wrote, "Oh how I hate to Get Up in the Morning." In his long life he composed more than 100 songs: "A Pretty Girl is like a Melody", "Blue Skies", "White Christmas", "God Bless America", "There's No Business Like Show Business", "Anything You Can Do", "This is the Army" and many more, plus scores for hit shows and movies: "Holiday Inn", "Annie Get Your Gun", "Easter Parade", etc.

In 1954 President Eisenhower presented him with a special gold medal for "God Bless America". In 1942 when I was stationed in Quantico Va. as a Navy Corpsman with the US Marines, Kate Smith performed for us and gave an inspiring rendition and had the whole auditorium of over a thousand men singing along with her. I felt that it should be our National Anthem.

Irving Berlin gave the Boy Scouts and Girl Scouts the royalties from, "God Bless America," and he gave his royalties from, "This is the Army," (approx. $10 million) to the US Government.

Life Magazine in 1970 called him one of the 100 most important Americans of the century.

CHAPTER TWENTY FIVE

BEVERLY SILLS

Coloratura Soprano & Guardian of Fine Arts

Beverly Sills

BORN MAY 15, 1929 IN N.Y. (Brooklyn) as Belle Miriam Silverman. Her father came from Romania and her mother from the Ukraine. As a young child under 7 years old she had memorized 22 arias and she sang them in Italian. She became one of American great coloratura sopranos with an international appeal. At 50 and at the top of her profession, she retired. She became the Director of the New York City Opera. In 1994 she was named Chairwoman of N.Y. City Lincoln Center. She is involved deeply in music and humanity betterment.

I suggest reading her autobiography, *"Bubble's a self portrait,"* published in 1977, in which she tells how she came to have been given that nick-name and her wonderful career that was touched with a some irony.

CHAPTER TWENTY-SIX

MILTON FRIEDMAN

Nobel Prize Winner

Milton & Rose Friedman

BORN IN BROOKLYN N.Y. of immigrant parents from Eastern Europe. During his childhood the family struggled financially, living above the store they ran. His father died when he was15. He graduated from high school at age 16. He received an under graduate degree from Rutgers, Masters from the Univ. of Chicago and a Doctorate from Columbia Univ. Influenced by the famous Arthur Burns. In 1938 he married fellow graduate student at the Univ. of Chicago, Rose Director. They have two children, Janet and David. In 1946 he joined the faculty of the Univ. of Chicago and remained there for 31 years. He became a leader in the Chicago School of Economics, rejecting John Maynard Keynes theories, i.e., "...only with heavy government spending could a nation prosper." He opposes bureaucratic welfare subsidies. An overly simple statement of his philosophy might be the old chestnut, "There is no such thing as a free lunch."

Friedman's primary premise is that the change in the nation's money supply can cause the economy to expand or wither, not government intervention. The Federal Reserve in 1930 permitted the money supply to decline by one third and a recession became The Great Depression. Read his: *A Monetary History of the U.S., 1867-1960-1963.*

In 1967 he received the Nobel Prize in Economic Science. In a special Fall issue, Life Magazine listed Friedman as one of the most important Americans of the 20th Century.

As of this writing, 88-year-old Friedman established the Milton and Rose Friedman Foundation for Education Choice.

The foundation shows his wish and love to improve the quality of our schools, whether government or private. He says "...a radical reconstruction of the educational system has the potential of staving off social conflict...(and) private enterprise (could gradually) enact in each state a voucher system that would enable parents to choose the schools...I first proposed such a voucher system 45 years ago... nothing else will force the (the public schools) to improve...(further consider) how competition from the Japanese transformed the domestic auto industry... Vouchers are not an end in themselves; they are a means to move the government to a market system. (And finally)...We shall not be willing to see a group of our population move into third world conditions..."

Milton Friedman Died, Nov.2006

CHAPTER TWENTY-SEVEN

DR. HERBERT L. NEEDLEMAN

Exposes a Seething Epidemic

Dr. Herbert Needleman

A MULTI-DISCIPLINED SCHOLAR, born 1927, BA from Muhlenberg College, Psychiatry from Temple University, Health Science Center and MD from University of Pennsylvania. Grew up in the Philadelphia area, graduating from Overbrook High School 1944. Now professor of Child Psychiatry and Pediatrics at University of Pittsburgh School of Medicine, where he developed a new method of measuring a child's body burden of the metal, lead. He initiated a large-scale study of intelligence and behavior of those with positive high lead quotients in bones and teeth.

His findings were alarming. He found in all races, that these individuals were prone to have low IQ's and a propensity for violent and bizarre behavior. Also those with high lead burden were four times more likely to have, "run-ins" with the law, i.e. be involved in arrests & adjudication.

I finally can lay blame to a cause when I see a young person with green/orange hair, body piercings – ears, tongue, navel, eye-lids etc, and/or tattoos. Maybe the suffering parents can be thankful because that behavior may take the place of more strident violence.

In some cases school districts pay more than three times the normal per student cost to transport and "teach" (warehouse) these damaged children in special schools. It is an epidemic, though an "arcane epidemic."

Back in the 1920s when "leaded gas" (additive tetraethyl lead) was introduced to improve performance and prevent knocks, the plant that produced the initial supply incurred a horrendous toll on the 40 workers; five died, others began hallucinating, some suffered from convulsions, some became permanently psychotic. Safeguards were initiated and production was increased. No "safeguards," were in place for what came out of the tail-pipes from the 1920s to 1980s. An "organic" form of lead rained on us, tons and tons of it for 60 odd years. Its residue is even now in the food chain.

Are we being confronted with a new toxin? Dr. Needleman warns, "MMT" additive, METHYLCYLOPENTA-DIENYL MANGANESE TRICABONYL may be the culprit. Dr. Needleman is concerned because high doses of "organic" manganese can cause neurological impairment similar to Parkinson's' Disease. Lead, manganese and other substances at the "organic" levels are toxic. That's the way they come out of the tail pipes. Dr. Needleman explains, "Organic form crosses the blood-brain barrier." Dr. Needleman may not be the John Wayne type, but he is a hero.

CHAPTER TWENTY EIGHT

EMMA LAZARUS

American Poet

Born in N.Y. July 22, 1849. Died in N.Y. November 19, 1887.

She is a poet most noted for writing, "The New Colossus" at The Statue of Liberty, 2nd verse:

"Keep, ancient lands, your storied pomp!"

Cries, she

With silent lips.

"Give me your tired, your poor,

Your huddled masses yearning to be free,

The wretched refuse of you teeming shore,

Send these, the homeless, tempest-tossed to me:

I left my lamp besides me the golden door."

Her great-grandfather arrived here even before the American Revolution.

Righteous Jews bios. to follow

CHAPTER TWENTY-NINE

UP BURTONS AND BREAK OUT

WELL INTO THE VOYAGE THERE was evidence that oil was leaking from some of the storage casks. Periodically water would be flushed into the holds where the whale oil was stored in wooden barrels. This had a dual purpose, first the water caused the wood to swell and thus tighten the staves seal and second, any leaking oil would show up when pumping it out. The solution was to shut down and have the casks hoisted on deck for examination and correction.

Starbuck went to Ahab's cabin to report the problem and he says, "The oil in the hold is leaking. We must up the Burtons and break out."

With this Ahab goes into a tirade. Only he is master! And to "heave to for a week to tinker a parcel of old hoops..." rather than pursue his main quest?

Starbuck then invokes Ahab's responsibility to the owners. Ahab retorts, "Thou art always prating me about the miserly owners...I am the only owner, Its Commander! Devil! Dost thou so much as dare to critically think of me? On deck!"

Starbuck politely replies, "Nay sir not yet; I do entreat...shall we not understand each better than hitherto Captain Ahab?" Ahab then seized a loaded musket from a rack and points it toward Starbuck... "There is one god that is Lord over the earth and one captain that is Lord over the Pequod! On deck!"

Starbuck goes to leave but stops and replies, "Thou hast outraged not insulted me, sir; but for that I ask thee not beware of Starbuck; thou wouldst but laugh; but let Ahab beware of Ahab; beware of thyself old man!" Then Starbucks leaves.

Ahab must have been affected by Starbuck's words, for going up on deck himself he gives orders to: "Furl t'gallant-sails and close-reef the top sails, fore and aft; break the main yard. Up Burtons, and break out the main hold." His orders were executed, the Burtons were hoisted and the task of bringing the casks out was begun. (*Burtons*, nautical tern for hoisting-tackle)

Starbucks invokes Ahab's responsibility to the owners and Ahab says: "I am the only real owner..." The media has both outraged and insulted us. Thou wouldst but laugh; but let Ahab beware of Ahab; Beware of thyself Old Man. Who really owns the air waves?

As one of the consequences of the Up Burtons order, Queequeg, Ishmael's great friend, was one of those assigned to work in the hold to move oil casks amid the miasmic dampness, mold and slime; there he caught a chill which brought on a fever. Confined to his hammock he grew faint, over time becoming almost a shadow of his former self.

Queequeg while in Nantucket had seen little canoes made of dark wood. He learned that they were used as coffins, not unlike the canoes of his homeland. He would prefer the coffin to being wrapped up in his hammock and dropped to the sharks. As he wished, the ship's carpenter took his measurements and made a coffin. Queequeg insisted on seeing it and trying it out and provisioning it with his treasured worldly possessions: the metal part of his harpoon, a paddle, from his boat, his carved wooden god, fresh water and biscuits. He was satisfied with it.

However; to everyone's surprise after that he began to rally and regain his health. He said that he changed his mind about dying because he had a little duty ashore to perform and that had to be done first. And after a few indolent days he was fit. The coffin became his sea chest for his clothes and possessions.

CHAPTER THIRTY

THE BLACKSMITH PERTH

PERTH IS THE SHIP'S BLACKSMITH, a man in his 60's. Why would a talented blacksmith leave the Town comforts and go to sea? He had owned property, a home and a forge, was married to a youthful loving wife, had three children, and went to church. To all, he was the very embodiment of order and success until... "One night under the cover of darkness and further concealed in the most cunning disguise, a desperate burglar slid into his happy home and robbed them all of everything. And darker yet to tell, the blacksmith himself did ignorantly conduct this burglar into his family's heart. It was the Bottle Conjurer! Upon opening that fatal cork, flew the fiend and shriveled up his home..."

When in time he had so embraced that bottle, wife, children, and business were forsaken so much so that his ruin was complete; wife, children in extreme poverty and malnutrition, all died, the property sold for debts. Only at this bottom when he could welcome death did the sea beckon and put him at the forge on the Pequod.

Well into the voyage, Ahab pays him a visit and remarks about the sparks caused by his hammering the red-hot metal, Ahab says, "...look here, they burn; but thou-thou liv'st among them without a scorch..." and he answers... "Because I am scorched all over, Captain Ahab. I am past scorching, not easily can'st thou scorch a scar."

Ahab continues his conversation with Perth and then discloses that he wants him to make a special harpoon for him, and he provides a bag of nail stubs from the steel shoes of a racing horse. Perth asks, "Is that not for the White Whale?" Ahab answers, "For the White Fiend! Here are my razors, the best steel and make the barbs as sharp as the needle-sheet of an Icy Sea."

Perth sets about working the items into a superb harpoon. He was about to give the barbs their final heat prior to tempering them and he asks Ahab to place the water cask near. Ahab says, "No, no, no water for that; I want it of true-death temper. Ahoy, there! Tashego, Queequeg, Daggoo. What say Pagans! Will you give me as much blood as will cover this barb?" They agree. The punctures were made in each flesh and the barbs were tempered in blood. Then in Latin Ahab says it is Baptized in the name of Satan, "Ego no Baptizo te in nominee patis, sed nominee diaboli."

Righteous Jews Continued

CHAPTER THIRTY-ONE

ROSALYN (SUSSMAN) YALOW

Nobel Prize Winner

BORN JULY 19,1921 IN N.Y. in the Bronx.

She was reading well before she entered kindergarten. She attended public schools and was advised to study science. She graduated from high school at age 15. At college she graduated Phi Beta Kappa and magna cum laude with a BA degree in physics and chemistry. Received a Ph.D. from the

Rosalyn (Sussman) Yalow

Univ. of Illinois, Urbania. After one year of work at the Federal Telecommunications Lab, she joined the faculty at Hunter College and later to the V.A. Hospital in the Bronx where the use of radioisotopes were studied for diagnosis and treatment of diseases. She and fellow scientist Dr. Solomon Berson produced a revolutionary method of radioimmunoassay, "RIA", a way to measure the amount of insulin in the blood of an adult diabetic. RIA use solved medical roadblocks in laboratories throughout the world. With RIA, blood collection centers now can prevent blood contaminated with hepatitis virus from being distributed.

She was the first American woman to receive a Nobel Prize in science and the second in medicine.

Because of RIA it is possible to measure concentrations of substances in the blood or other fluids.

CHAPTER THIRTY-TWO

MICHAEL MEDVED

American Rational Philosopher

Michael Medved

HE BECAME WELL KNOWN as a film critic, co-host of, "Sneak Previews." Other facets of Medved's career give him high ratings as an author: *Hollywood vs. America, The Shadow Presidents,* and one he wrote with his wife Diane Medved, *Saving Childhood*-protecting our children from the national assault on innocence. He authored several other books.

Born in Philadelphia October 3, 1948 to David and Renate (Rosa) Medved. His father, David, a Navy veteran, held a Ph.D. in physics and was a candidate for scientific astronaut. Michael was raised in San Diego after the family moved there and remained there from the first through tenth grade. He was an undergraduate at Yale at age 16. Later as a graduate student he embraced the liberal-left and was involved in anti-war protest.

He received a draft deferment by part-time teaching 7th and 8th grades 3 hours a day.

While at Yale Law School his classmates included Hillary and Bill Clinton. Before that, as an undergraduate, among his classmates were (had been) Senator John Kerry of Mass., Gov. George Pataki of N.Y., Pres. of U.S. George W. Bush, and Gov. Tony Knowles of Alaska.

In 1985 he married Diane Elvenstar. They have three children: Sarah Julia, Shaya Elana, and Daniel Joshua.

Radio Talk-Show host to1.8 million listeners in 118 markets, where he captivates an intelligent throng of listeners with his common sense rationale. I was especially smitten with an innovative "role-playing" he did during the Presidential Campaign where he gave the responses of the various candidates of all political persuasions to questions as they would more than likely have replied.

In 1971 he served as a campaign consultant to Rep. Ron Dellums whom he now terms, as "As Stalinist Democrat from California." After six weeks Michael resigned in disgust. The experience helped push him away from the Left. In 1979 writing and researching the critically acclaimed book, "*The Shadow Presidents,*" a history of the White House Chiefs of Staff, completed his transformation from Liberal to Conservative.

Some of his other books included: *What Happened to The Class of '65, Hospital,* co-authored with Harry Medved, *50 Worst Films of all Time, Golden Turkey Award* and *The Hollywood Hall of Shame.*

Back to our Sea-Saga: (Righteous Jews bios to follow)

CHAPTER THIRTY-THREE

AHAB AND FEDALLAH -THE PARSEE

AFTER AHAB BAPTIZES HIS harpoon, the Pequod continues and more whales are taken. Fedallah, a mystic, also called The Parsee, is Ahab's harpooner, confidant and private prophet. They are together when the Parsee makes a calming but oblique prophesy for Ahab. It is not too unlike Shakespeare's Mac Beth when the witches give the prophetic conundrum, "Be lion mettled, proud, and take no kare who chafes, who frets, or where conspirers are. Mac Beth shall never vanquished be till mighty Birnam Wood to high Dunsiname hill shall come against three, ... (and none of woman born shall kill thee) ...."

Ahab and the Parsee and the whale-boat crew have been out all night, having had a successful chase. The whale carcass is tethered and a lantern hangs atop a waif-pole that had been thrust into the dead whales' spout hole. They wait for the Pequod. The men still sleep, only Ahab and the Parsee are now awake. Ahab just awakened says, *"I have dreamed it again."*

"Of the hearses? Have I not said, old man, that neither hearse nor coffin can be thine?"

"And who are hearsed that die on the sea?"

"But I said, old man, that ere thou couldst die on this voyage, two hearses must verily be seen by thee on the sea; the first not made by mortal hands; and the visible wood of the last one must be grown in America,"

"Aye, aye? A strange sight that, Parsee: --hearse and its plumes floating over the ocean with the waves for the pallbearers. Ha! Such a sight we shall not soon see."

"Believe it or not, thou canst not die till it be seen, old man."

"And what was that saying about thyself?"

"Though it come to the last, I shall still go before thee thy pilot."

"And when thou art so gone before – if that ever befall – then ere I can follow, thou must still appear to me, to pilot me still? –Was it not so? Well, then did I believe all ye say, oh my pilot! I have here two pledges that I shall yet slay Moby Dick and survive it."

"Take another pledge, old man," said Parsee, as his eye lighted up like fire-flies in the gloom – "Hemp only can kill thee."

CHAPTER THIRTY-FOUR

ALBERT EINSTEIN

The 20th Century's Most Famous Physicist

Albert Einstein

BORN IN 1879 IN ULM, GERMANY. Died in 1955. Became 20th century's most famous physicist. His parents weren't observant Jews but as an adult he did believe in a supreme intelligence.

He won the Nobel Prize for physics in 1921. He had left school in Germany in 1894 at the age of 15 and went to Italy with his parents. He continued his studies in Switzerland, graduating at the age of 21 in physics and mathematics. He wanted to teach, but being Jewish and not a Swiss citizen, he was a turned down. He accepted a minor job in the patent office in Bern.

He revolutionized scientific thought during the seven years he worked as a patent examiner, through his inquires of time and gravity. His theories at this time were beginning to take shape to become the foundation for modern science.

While still working at the patent office, he married Mileva Marec, also a student of physics. They had 3 children: 2 sons and a daughter. His famous equation $E=mc^2$ changed physicists' understanding of the world. Time and space are a continuum.

Einstein was named in1909 to be an adjunct professor at the Swiss University. of Zurich and later full professor at the German University in Prague. He later became professor at the Prussian Academy of Science at Berlin. He went on to propound mathematical and rational theories.

Though Einstein was opposed to violence, ironically he is credited for helping to bring about the nuclear age. He believed that a great deal of energy could be liberated by the conversion of a small amount of mass. In 1934, Nazis confiscated his property and citizenship. By escaping to the United States and accepting a position at the institute for Theoretical Physics in Princeton, New Jersey, he escaped the horrors that were to come. He became an American citizen in 1940.

In 1939 he wrote to President Roosevelt, representing himself and other scientists, that it was now possible to release atomic energy. His letter led to the secret project, with America being first to introduce atomic weapons.

CHAPTER THIRTY-FIVE

RITA LEVI-MONTALCINI

Nobel Prize in Medicine

RITA LEVI-MONTALCINI WAS BORN in Turin, Italy in 1909. As a young woman she wanted to study medicine after the death by cancer of her former governess. She graduated from medical school in1936, specializing in neutrology. The fascist government in 1938 barred Jews from university posts and forbade them from practicing medicine. She was dismissed from her post at the institute of Anatomy and the Neurology clinic.

In spite of W.W.II and the need to change location, she continued her research with chicken embryos. She made a discovery: "Nerve Growth Factor" (NGF). The discovery has far reaching effect for such diseases as Parkinson and Alzheimer's, which attack the nervous system, finding a relationship between the nerve cells and the immune system.

Dr. Levi-Montalcini came to the Zoology department at Washington Univ. in St. Louis. After the war she remained there for 30 years, and became an American citizen in 1956. She retained dual citizenship as an Italian and became president of the Institute of Italian Encyclopedia.

CHAPTER THIRTY-SIX

BEN STEIN

A man of all Seasons

Ben Stein

BENJAMIN STEIN, BORN NOVEMBER 1944 in Washington D.C., son of economist and writer, Herbert Stein. He graduated from Columbia University in 1966, with honors, and from Yale Law School in 1970 as valedictorian. He worked as a poverty lawyer and later a trial lawyer in trade regulation at the Federal Trade Commission. He taught political and social content of mass cultures.

In 1973 and 1974 he was a speechwriter for Nixon and Ford. He was a columnist and editorial writer for the Wall Street Journal and for King Features Syndicate and Barrons, where his articles about the ethics of management buyouts and issues of fraud in the Milken Drexel junk bond scheme drew national attention.

He also writes for Los Angeles Magazine, New York Magazine, 'E,' Online, and a thing I read in every issue of the American Spectator, 'Ben Steins Diary'. He's written and published 16 books, 7 novels, and 9 nonfiction about finance, about ethical social issue in finance and also about the political and social content of mass culture. His titles include: *A License to Steal, Michael Milken and the Conspiracy to Bilk the Nation, The View from Sunset Boulevard* and others. He is an actor in movies, TV, and commercials. Starting in 1997 he has been the host of "Comedy Central" quiz show, and "Win Ben Stein's Money". He lives with wife Alexandra Denman (lawyer,) his son Tommy and lots of pets in Los Angeles.

CHAPTER THIRTY-SEVEN

EDWARD TELLER

America's Science Sentinel

EDWARD TELLER WAS BORN in Budapest, Hungary on January 15, 1908. He received University training in Germany, and has a Ph.D. in physics from the University of Leipzig.

In 1934 he served as a lecturer at the University of London under auspices of the Jewish rescue committee. In1933 he came to the United States, held a professorship at George Washington University and in 1941 became a United States citizen.

During WWII he joined the Manhattan Project. His efforts included work on the first nuclear reactor and calculations of the effects of a fission explosion and research on a potential fusion reaction.

Teller received the Albert Einstein award, the Enrico Fermi award, the Harvey Prize from Technion-Israel Institute, and the National Medal of Science.

He has a great concern for civil defense since the 1950's, and is a senior research fellow at the Hoover Institute, where he is specializing in international and national policies of defense and energy.

Books he has written: *Conversations on the Dark Secrets of Physics Better a Shield Than a Sword, Pursuit of Simplicity* and *Energy from Heaven and Earth.*

CHAPTER THIRTY-EIGHT

LINA STERN

Breached the Blood Brain Barrier

LINA STERN, SHE REVIVED the dead. Born in 1878 in Lithuania, Russia. She died 1968.

She was the first woman admitted to the Soviet Academy of Sciences. She wrote more than 400 works on medical physiological topics. She pioneered in physiological processes in humans, especially of the central nervous system. To the outside world, work as a woman and a Jew were minimized by communist Russia.

She had worked in Geneva, Switzerland, but returned to Russia. During the war she overcame the blood (hematoencephalic) barrier. She gave brain injections to 338 patients given up for dead and found 301 recovered. Her treatment then became the protocol in Soviet hospitals. She was a graduate of the University of Geneva in Switzerland.

Righteous Jews will be continued

CHAPTER THIRTY-NINE

THE LIFE BUOY

WHEN A SAILOR ON WATCH from the main mast as a lookout for whales falls into the sea a life buoy (preserver) is thrown to him but it is so rotted that it will not float. The seaman is lost. Starbuck accepts a suggestion that Queequeg's coffin would make a good but odd life buoy, and has the carpenter caulk it and make it seaworthy for that purpose. When Ahab sees the coffin/life buoy he thinks such a dichotomy may be an ominous sign but is not sure. Here Melville drops any semblance of Ahab's rationality when Ahab decides to consult Pip on the matter.

CHAPTER FORTY

LISE MEITNER

She Opened the Curtain on the Nuclear Era

LISE MEITNER, BORN IN 1878, died in 1968. She was a physicist, and did work on atomic fission, but fled to Sweden due to the ensuing Nazi threat. As a Swedish citizen she worked for the Nobel Institute and the Atomic Energy Laboratory. Without her work the secret of nuclear fission may not have been revealed when it was. Her partner, Dr. Otto Hahn, received the Nobel Prize for the effort.

Early in her career during WWI she served as a nurse, though she had her doctorate from the University of Vienna in physics, because in the past, women just didn't become physicists, but she gave her services. In 1946 she came to the United States as a visiting professor for a year at the Catholic University in Washington. She is a co-recipient of the American Atomic Energy Commission's Enrico Fermi Award.

More Righteous Jews will follow

CHAPTER FORTY-ONE

THE QUADRANT

NOW THE PEQUOD IS IN THAT Japanese sea on a clear, sun-soaked day. Ahab's quadrant, including colored glasses to sight the solar fire to take a reading and get a fix of the ship's position, is handed to him. With astrological-looking instruments to his eyes he remains in that position some moments to catch the precise instant when the sun gains a precise meridian. Ahab soon calculates what his latitude is at that moment. Ahab says, "Thou sea mark! Thou high and mighty Pilot! Thou tellest me truly where we are but canst thou cast the least hint where I shall be? ...Where is Moby Dick? ..."

Then gazing at his quadrant mutters, "Foolish toy...play thing of haughty admirals...commodore and captains...curse thee thou vain toy...curse thee thou quadrant!" dashing it to the deck, "no longer will I guide my earthly way by thee...thus I trample on thee thou paltry thing...thus I spit and destroy thee!"

Trample and destroy the quadrant, abide with your own dead reckoning. Do without astronomical observations. These refer to man-made guides, but they could correspond to the spiritual guides, i.e. the Ten Commandments, the Talmud, and the New Testaments and other inspired writings, The Words of God, Harken back to Fathers Marple's sermon, "We must obey God, not ourselves...otherwise it could mean being swallowed by our own folly, being led by our's and not God's Will must result in our destruction."

Shortly, almost out of a clear sky, the deadly thunder roars. Towards evening of that day the Pequod is torn of her canvas. Ahab's own boat is stove in. They are in a typhoon.

Starbuck points out to Stubb that the typhoon is pushing the ship off the direction Ahab had set, "the better to head for home," but Ahab reappears and addresses the crew midst the thunder rain and lighting.

The three masts attract an unconsummated form of an electrical phenomenon where the light charges down and glows between the attractions. The crew called it "corposants" also called St. Elmo's fire.

Ahab, in defiance of the storm and a pending mutiny, brandishes his harpoon above his head as it, too, emits fiery pulses, saying, "Aye, Aye, men! Look at it! Mark it well! The white flame but lights the way to the white whale...All your oaths to hunt the white whale are as binding as mine...heart, soul, body, lungs, and life..."

Those of the crew who had expressed doubts and mistrust were now silent and in awe and Ahab is unhurt.

The electric fire display would rival any special effects that Hollywood might contrive and there cannot be a replay button nor editing. Ahab was not a stranger to lightening. The scar that ran from his head to his toes attests to it and during the tempest he says, "I bear the scar..."

Encyclopedia Britannica: "'St. Elmo's Fire' is a very beautiful eerie form of atmosphere electricity that usually appears in stormy weather around church spires, sailing masts and airplane wings."

Capt. Ahab goes below. Later as the storm abates Starbuck goes to inform Ahab and he comes upon a rack of loaded muskets. Ahab once used one to threaten Starbuck's life. Starbuck knows that the lives of all are endangered by this madman's quest and here he has a chance to kill Ahab or put him in chains and save the crew and ship, but he cannot bring himself to do the deed. He isn't aware that by not taking some action he is consigning all to death except Ishmael.

CHAPTER FORTY-TWO

ROSALIND E. FRANKLIN

Opened the Door to DNA Discovery

ROSALIND E. FRANKLIN, born 1920, to an English-Jewish family, died 1958. She was a scientist. Her description of the probable DNA structure, containing deoxyribonucleic acid, which is the key to heredity, made it a lot easier for James D. Watson and Francis H. Crick and their discovery of DNA. It was her X-ray photograph of DNA that helped Watson and Crick unravel DNA secrets. Unfortunately she died before she could have added more to the study.

CHAPTER FORTY-THREE

THE RENOWNED JEWISH FAMILIES SOME WITH MEDIA CONNECTIONS

ANY ATTEMPT TO SUM UP in a paragraph or two and do justice to any of the following extraordinary Jewish families cannot be done. Therefore you may read, *"Great Jewish Families,"* and a lot can be gleaned from the internet, especially their foundations. I'm impressed by their contributions to our country and to civilization in general and part and parcel goes to their philanthropy. Some of it favors Jewish charities but many lavish the fortunes on both; a few devote most of their largess to the general welfare of the whole of society.

One might be tempted to paraphrase Winston Churchill's remark about the RAF in Britain's darkest hour, "never were so many indebted to so few when it comes to Jewish contribution in the last 100+ years in our country. Unfortunately, there too is a negative side. I'm not referring only to obvious criminals like Myer Lansky, Bugsy Segal nor Michael Milken and Marc Rich etc. But more to those who splay out their "legal" crimes against humanity through media and legal controlled substances. What costs society has incurred from birth defects, premature birth, destroyed families and lives, crime and destruction of ethical standards will never be calculated.

THE BRONFMANS

This family has been a force worldwide. Its founder, Yechiel Bronfman, owned a tobacco plantation in Bessarabia, a former Romanian province, before he came to Canada in 1889. In

Canada he found the hotel business to his liking. One of his four sons, Samuel, went into the liquor business and later in 1928 he bought the old distillery firm of Joseph E. Seagram and sons. His brothers joined him and contributed to making it one of the world's greatest enterprises and the world's largest distiller.

In time Samuel bought out his brothers' and their offsprings' interest in the firm so that he could leave the business to his two sons, Edgar and Charles.

Edgar went on to succeed his father. His brother Charles was active in the firm for some time, but he is best known for the ownership of the Montreal Expos and the many charities he supported.

Edgar is now a naturalized US citizen. He improved the company's strength in part by investing its funds outside of the liquor industry. At one time Seagram owned 14.99% of the media, entertainment giant Time Warner Inc. They became the largest private landowners in Canada. They own Tropicana Products (fruit juice), many large shopping malls, and owned nearly 25% of Du Pont, the Parent Co. of Conoco Oil and held blocks of stocks in other energy companies.

Forbes magazine lists Edgar as one of the 400 richest persons in the country. In 1995 he was worth just under $3 billion.

In semi-retirement he is devoted to Jewish charities, president of the World Jewish Congress. He was influential in getting Russia to permit a sizable Jewish "exodus" to USA, Israel and other places. He is representing the Jewish people and other claims against Swiss banks that may be holding money belonging to Holocaust victims. He was also known for being instrumental in uncovering former UN secretary Kurt Walheim's Nazi past.

Edgar Bronfman's son (Edgar Jr.) now runs the company. It is said that at his urging, much of the Dupont stock was sold so that he could raise $5.7 billion to buy MCA, a huge multi-media Hollywood conglomerate that is into recording, video, C.D.'s, publishing, Universal Pictures, and much more.

Edgar Jr. always moved in media/entertainment circles, and this gamble was in line with that. He is also on the board of trustees of public broadcasting affiliate WNET NY and appointed White House advisory for export by Bill Clinton.

Famous Jewish Families in Media continued

The Selznicks

Lewis Joseph Selznick, founder, came from the Ukraine, Russia. He came to USA possibly in the 1890's and went into the jewelry business. On moving to NY City he became a producer of silent motion pictures and prospered. Son Myron became president of one of his father's motion picture companies and was steeped in the business. Another son more widely known as David O. Selznick was a great producer with famous pictures to his credit such as "Gone with the Wind", "Spellbound", and many others.

The Paleys

Samuel Paley came from the Ukraine, Russia in 1875. Died in America in 1963. He was quite a successful businessman as a cigar manufacturer of the well known brand "La Palina."

Samuel's son William, born in 1901 died in 1990. William invested in a budding industry that would become CBS. With financial aid from his father, he controlled the firm and became the president and later chairman of the Radio and TV giant.

The Newhouses

Samuel Newhouse born in 1895, died August 1979, founder of a media enterprise whose value in the mid 1990's was $9 billion. His brothers Norman and Theodore joined the business, as did their sons.

Through their holding company, Advance Publications, they owned about 30 newspapers, Cleveland Plain dealer, Newark Star, Ledger, New Yorker, andmany more including Vanity Fair, Vogue and several radio and 99 TV stations. Also many cities have two "competing" papers under their ownership. The publishing conglomerate Random House and all its subsidiaries belong to them.

Their charities go both to Jewish and non-Jewish organizations. Newhouse's wealth was said to be in the billions and probably the wealthiest Jewish family in the USA.

The Warners

The name "Warner Bros" was begun when Harry M. Warner born in Poland in 1881, died in L.A. in 1958. Brother Albert (Abe) born US, brother Samuel Louis born US 1887 and brother Jack born 1892 in Canada died in the USA 1978. Jack's only son Jack Jr. born USA 1916 died in 1995 in LA was an executive in Warner Bros. To name a few of Warner Bros. Films- "The Maltese Falcon", "Casablanca", "My Fair Lady" etc.

The Annenebergs

Almost from the beginning after Moses Anneneberg came to this country from East Prussia he was involved through Hearst publishing with periodical circulation. Later, on his own, he acquired and begun publishing the Daily Racing Forum, the Phila. Inquirer and the Holding Co., Triangle Publication. He was a tough competitor and critic of the policies of the New Deal Administration. This was to cause him great personal suffering and the near demise of his enterprises.

His only son, Walter, took over and kept things going. Not only did it survive but after time, flourished. He added Radio and TV stations, the TV guide and magazine, "Seventeen" and under the Nixon/Ford Presidency 1968/1974 he was ambassador to Great Britain. He created the Anneneberg Foundation, an organization designed for total usefulness to all of society, especially in the field of communications, and generously supports Art Museums and Educational and Health Institutions.

This extract is from internet htpp://www.whannenberg.org: "The Anneneberg Foundation is the successor corporation to the

Anneneberg School at Radnor, Pennsylvania established in 1958 by Walter H. Anneneberg. It exists to advance the public well-being through improved communication. As the principal means of achieving its goal, the foundation encourages the development of more effective ways to share ideas and knowledge."

The foundation generally limits grants to those likely to produce beneficent change on a large scale. It is open to collaboration with other philanthropic institutions.

Mr. Walter H. Anneneberg died at the age of 94 as I was in the midst of my writing on October 1, 2002.

CHAPTER FORTY-FOUR

INDEPENDENTS & AND SCRIPPS-HOWARD

NEWS AND ENTERTAINMENT DISSEMINATION organs, though mostly owned or controlled by Jews, are not monolithic. There are substantial media giants with a diffusion of ownership and views and they aren't always chaste.

They may include: Belo Corp., owns 4 daily papers in Seattle, Washington; Phoenix, Arizona; Rhode Island and Texas along with 19 TV stations. Gannett, an international corporation, operates in 44 states, D.C. Guam, U.K., Belgium, Germany, Italy and Hong Kong, having 100 daily papers, 700 non-dailies, 22 TV stations, revenue $6.4 billion – profit $1.16 billion in 2002. Misc. Hearst-Argyle, Knight-Ridder, Rupert Murdock News Corp., Sony Corp., Chicago Tribune, and Scripps-Howard.

The last, Scripps-Howard has a commonality with earlier mentioned media organizations because it was started in part by a family of immigrant (gentile) Christians from England. Though the founder, Edward W. Scripps (1854-1926) was born here, his siblings that helped him were born in England. Edward started the press empire in 1878 with the "Penny Press" with a loan from his half brother, James. The Penny Press today is the "Cleveland Press." Brother James founded the "Detroit News" in 1873.

Edward W. was inordinately careful with funds, but expansive in creating more news outlets. He bought cheap news print and used presses operated at "bare-bones" costs, but on a personal level he was a bombastic, cigar-chumping, imbibing social lion.

His older half sister, Ellen Browning Scripps (1836-1932), was a brilliant person in her own right. She was a teacher while still a teenager, later graduated from Knox College. She was a profound influence on his life and on the business. She invested her time writing a lively column on people and affairs. She helped her brother in founding other papers and invested her savings in them. She had a keen business sense and became wealthy, but later was the recipient of a large legacy from another brother, making her very wealthy. She felt her fortune was entrusted to her "for the benefit of humanity." When she retired in 1896 in the La Jolla area of San Diego, she gave away millions to schools, hospitals, YMCA and YWCA's, churches of several denominations and the following institutions: The Public Library, Scripps Memorial Hospital, Woman's Club, Bishop's school, Metabolic Clinic, Scripps Institute of Oceanography, Natural History Museum, The Zoo and it's research lab in Balboa Park, Community House Playground, and gifts to Pomona and Claremont Colleges.

At one time the company published 400 newspapers serving 25 million readers. The company motto, "Give light and the people will find the way."

Today there are 21 daily newspapers and 10 broadcasting outlets, 3 cable and one satellite outlet. In 1996 the larger part of their cable systems were sold.

The "Howard" in Scripps-Howard came about in the 1920s when Roy Howard, a newsman, rose to become the president. In 1950 Scripps started publishing Charles Schultz comic strip, "Peanuts," Snoopy and Charlie Brown. Soon it was carried by 2,000 newspapers around the globe. There's a lot more to the Scripps story. Check the Internet.

To say that the above "Independents" are not influenced by the dominantly managed media outlets would be incorrect.

Virtually all sit-coms, made for TV movies and features are produced by Hollywood or by their surrogates here and abroad. To fill all the hours of broadcasting, aside from "news" is a daunting task. To fill it with wholesome, profitable fare is Herculean. It is easier to buy shows already packaged and sell advertising around them, than to create fresh, "masterpieces." Even shows with long dead stars are sold and resold for years and years; note "I Love Lucy," "The Honeymooners," "All in the Family," "MASH" and others. The secondary marketing goes on and on. The same unfortunately can be said of porn and no stars are needed. Any male and female prostitutes will do.

The competition is fearsome. The heydays of the three big networks are dwindling. Literally, there are thousands of cable and satellite channels in the wings readying for a seat in a rabid game of musical chairs.

Many outlets by default or design have gravitated to various faces of porn. Cheap "packages" that will guarantee viewers, revenue and indoctrination.

Also both the written and the electronic media outlets can be slaves to the wire services that will to reflect their own agendas.

Renowned Jewish families will continue after the following:

> *Assuredly, I say to you,*
> *Whatever you bind on earth*
> *Will be bound in heaven and*
> *Whatever you loose on earth*
> *Will be loosed in heaven*
>
> Matthew 18-18

CHAPTER FORTY-FIVE

JOHNNY APPLESEED & POST-MORTEM.

THE MORE YOU READ MOBY DICK, the more you feel that Ishmael is Melville. The author and his character's philosophy coalesce.

When Ishmael opens his heart and soul on leaving the Seaman's Chapel in New Bedford, I h ad what was perhaps a whimsical notion on my part; what if Ishmael met Johnny Appleseed, the folk hero, legend, and American Icon. Actually he was a real person named Jon Chapman. Melville and Chapman were contemporaries. Melville would have been about 26 years old when Chapman died in 1845 at age 71.

Johnny Appleseed (Chapman) had an extraordinary life, a pioneer, frontiersman, respected by Indians and settlers alike. To some he appeared eccentric, but he was well educated and a master orchardsman who laid out apple orchards in settlements and in the wildernesses. His long treks took him through what are now several Midwest states. He planted hundreds of apple orchards that benefited generations with the nourishing fruit that stored well, helping to sustain families through the long frontier winters. Yes, he carried sacks of apple seeds on these extensive travels along with the inspired words of God. The settlers of those times welcomed travelers, especially if they brought news or mail. Johnny Appleseed approaching a settler's cabin always announced, "Good news from Heaven!" And for those who could read he would leave a page or more of the holy writings. It worked like a lending library; he gave and exchanged the pages as he came and returned. For those without a reading skill and the young, he would read to them and sermonize. This gentle useful soul touched many lives and may have influenced the early moral endowments of those regions. Indeed a good media.

At this point I'd like to call Ishmael to repeat his sentiments expressed on leaving the Seaman's Chapel, i.e., "Me thinks my body is but the less of my better being... In fact, take my body who will, take it, I say it is not me." Johnny Appleseed would agree. Is it possible that Melville and Chapman shared the same theological mentor? I know Johnny Appleseed's.

Back in 1941 when I was to be a Navy Medical Corpsman, we were required to attend Post Mortems. At the first autopsy the pathologist in removing organs and parts explained their function and named them in a matter-of-fact manner, much like an auto shop class teacher in high school as he disassembles a car engine, but without the blood splattered gown, mask, gloves and the exposed thoracic/abdominal cavities.

As a 17-year old, this first experience gave me pause. I said to one of my fellow students, "Why, that's just the shell of a man!"

Now as I consider Ishmael's words and my innate reaction at the Post Mortem and what I know of the theology of Johnny Appleseed and reflect that a "shell" is a vessel, a receptacle that had held life, or a chrysalis that is shucked off when earthly use ends. A different form emerges, perhaps a more beautiful and perfect one? Perhaps not?

What if, in the world beyond, there is a period of "culling and rendering" the facades, the superficial, the trappings and the only thing left would be <u>You</u> with your ruling loves. The real <u>You</u>. On reaching such a juncture could there by any duplicity? Everything is out. Your face, body, clothes, walk, talk would tell all who you are and what you're about. You would then be the embodiment of your loves. And as all the "trappings – embellishments, duplicity, are vastly removed, to be alive you are then the truly living form of your loves. As such you'll gather with others that share the same or similar life (loves).

Could you be comfortable any other way? Or would you be uncomfortable, even in agony if you were forced to live contrary to your loves? What if, "After death man remains to eternity in the state of that life which he acquired for himself in the world."

It is something to think about.

The postmortem left me holding an insight I've held over the years; what if our bodies, eyes, taste, limbs, brain, bones, sinew, et al. constitute but our shell, a house we've leased where we reside during our visit here.

Isn't it incumbent that we honor it, keep it healthy and clean, orderly useful and not abuse, debase or degrade it because we're not done with it really.

Renowned Jewish Families continued (Some Media Connectons)

CHAPTER FORTY-SIX

THE GUGGENHEIMS

THE GUGGENHEIMS IMMIGRATED from Switzerland in 1847 and settled in Philadelphia, Pa. Patriarch, Simon Meyer Guggenheim (1792-1869), was a tailor, his only son, Meyer (1828-1905) established the family business in manufacturing and merchandising. Starting as a peddler, later an importer manufacturer of Swiss laces and embroideries. Meyer had eight sons and three daughters. Of the 7 surviving sons, four joined him in the expanding and profitable lace business.

In spite of the success he was enjoying, he took a gamble and bought controlling interest in some lead and silver mines near Leadville, Colorado. The move led to a bonanza that would become the Guggenheim Empire for gold, silver and copper. They phased out the lace business and concentrated on mining, smelting and refining while continuing expansion, gaining control of the American Smelting and Refining Co. (ASARCO). In effect the family ran the mining industry in the U.S.

One of his sons, Daniel (1856-1930), expanded further to tin mines in Bolivia, gold and copper in Alaska, diamonds in Africa, copper and nitrate in Chile. Virtually all the progeny were super achievers and contributed to the success over several generations.

Beyond the fabulous wealth they amassed, they also used their incredible energies for philanthropic, scientific, patriotic, intellectual and artistic endeavors.

One of Meyer's sons, Benjamin (1865-1912), who was active till his retirement in 1901, died assisting others into lifeboats, giving his life jacket to a woman. He was a passenger on the S.S. Titanic April 15, 1912.

The now famous generous Guggenheim Fellowship for the use of scholars and artists to study, travel with few restrictions are given yearly to citizens from the U.S., Canada, Philippines and other countries, after Simon (1867-1941), sixth son of Meyer, established it to honor a son of his who died early in life, "John Simon Memorial Foundation."

One of Daniel's sons, Robert (1885-1959) served as U. S. Ambassador to Portugal 1953-54. Another son, Harry Frank (1891-1971) promoted aeronautics and rocketry and publishing. Daniel's daughter Gladis Eleanor (1895-1980) married Roger W. Straus, a scion of the owners of Macy's department store chain. Their son Roger W. Straus Jr. became a major literary publisher, i.e. Farrar, Straus and Giroux.

More on Daniel's son, Harry Frank Guggenheim. His life achievements epitomized the Guggenheim epoch: He became a U.S. Navel Officer in aviation in both world wars. Gave Guggenheim grants for rocket research by Robert Goddard. Set up a foundation to improve human relations which included a study of women in the Israeli Kibbutzim. Also research promoting prehistoric studies in Africa by Dr. Leakey.

As president of the Daniel Guggenheim Fund, he promoted the development for commercial passenger travel by air. In a 1926 project, financial aid made the nationwide tour of the Richard E. Byrd North Pole Plane possible. He served on an aircraft carrier in the Pacific during WWII and was promoted to Capt. Back in 1929 he was ambassador to Cuba. He was active in civic affairs in New York. After the death of Uncle Solomon he completed the <u>Museum</u>, originally called the Solomon R. Guggenheim museum. He was married three times, the last one to Alicia Patterson, daughter of the founder of the New York Daily News and great granddaughter to the founder of the Chicago Tribune. He generously endowed universities, establishing aeronautical schools at Columbia, Princeton, Cornell and a jet propulsion lab at Caltech in Pasadena, and authored a book on aviation and International relations.

CHAPTER FORTY-SEVEN

THE OCHS AND SALZBERGERS

JULIUS OCHS (1826-1888) born in Bavaria.

At an early age he could speak English, German, French and Italian and while still young he left Bavaria for the United States. He joined family members in Kentucky. He married Bertha Levy, also from Bavaria, in 1855. They had six children. Three were sons, Adolph Simon, George Washington and Melton Barlow. During the Civil War, Julius was commissioned a Captain in the Ohio Volunteers. After the War he and his family moved to Knoxville, Tennessee. One of his sons, Adolph Simon Ochs (1858-1935) at the tender age of eleven years, started working at a newspaper, The Knoxville Chronicle. By age 19 years he started his own paper, The Chattanooga Dispatch, that failed.

A year later with the sum of $6,750 he attained controlling interest in the Chattanooga Times. He developed it into a successful paper. Also he founded a business periodical, The Tradesman. It was at this time that his father, Julius joined him and became the treasurer of the Chattanooga Times. By 1883 Adolph Simon was married to Effie Miriam Wise. They had only one child, a girl, Iphigene Bertha Ochs.

Adolph was interested in the New York market. He was aware that the New York Times was in serious financial trouble. This was in 1896. With $75,000 of borrowed money he took the troubled paper over and became its publisher. In time he brought it back to health and it became the most respected newspaper in the country with the motto: "All the news that's fit to print." This motto is still carried on the masthead today. It was his aim to rise above the scandal-touting papers of his day.

The paper has received 110 Pulitzer Prizes; its reporters received them while employed there but the record is not without its blemishes: The Pulitzer Prize winning journalist, Walter Duranty accepted the prize at a time when he was proven a blatant apologist of the mass murderer Stalin. Between 7 and 10 million Ukrainians were deliberately starved to death so that Stalin's brand of communism could prosper. Walter Duranty only wrote glowing reports from Moscow. In the New York Times on the 31st, March 1933, he writes, "Any report of a famine is an exaggeration or malignant propaganda." At this time the famed writer, journalist Malcolm Muggeridge, worked for the Manchester Guardian in the Ukraine. His reports about the great famine of 1932-1933 were both factual and accurate. He assessed Walter Duranty as, "...the greatest liar of any journalist I have ever met."

The above was excerpted from the Internet as reported by The Association of Ukrainians in Great Britain. They have been campaigning for the posthumous revocation of Duranty's 1932 Pulitzer Prize.

And another "blemish" has just occurred: the case of Time's reporter, Jayson Blair, the plagiarizer and fabricator who plied these deceits over a period of five years. He hoodwinked the readers and the management. Was it the case of one bamboozler slipping between the cracks, or could it be blamed on the New York Times obsession for diversity, affirmative action, political correctness, or were they afraid of the Union, or could they dare fire an Afro-American?

Back to the Ochs and the Salzbergers. Adolph Simon Ochs continues to acquire publications and with the help of his family, they were all arranged smoothly. He always insisted that he was not for the Zionist movement, not looking for a homeland. In effect he said, "Religion only makes me Jewish."

Adolph's only child, a daughter, "Iphigene," married Arthur Hays Salzberger (1891-1968). He came from a family of scholars and lawyers. When Adolph Simon Ochs died in 1935, the New York Times' ownership passed from the Ochs to the Salzbergers. Arthur Hays Salzberger took the reins and tried to maintain most of Adolph's policies. Under the Salzberger leadership the company expanded and acquired more media properties. After a series of health problems, his activities were reduced and his daughter Marian's husband, Orvil E. Dryfoos, took over. However, in 1963 Orvil died and Arthur Hays Salzberger's son Arthur Ochs Salzberger took the helm. The older Salzberger remained as chairman of the board until his death in 1968.

Again in 1992, Arthur Ochs Salzberger turned it over to his son, Arthur Ochs Salzberger Jr.

The New York Times company's revenues in 2002 were $3.11 billion. They publish the New York Times, The Boston Globe, The Internet Herald Tribune. They publish 16 other newspapers. They own 8 network affiliated TV stations, and 2 radio stations in New York.

The New York Times Company is listed in the New York stock exchange.

CHAPTER FORTY-EIGHT

JOSEPH PULITZER

(1847-1911)

Joseph Pulitzer

IN THE INITIAL RESEARCH to write a mini-bio on Joseph Pulitzer to add another name to the Jewish-media standouts, I was stopped in my tracks. He was born the son of a wealthy Jew in Hungary in 1847, but with a devout Christian mother. Yet he was an extraordinary man who had some claim to Jewish heredity.

Were he not from a wealthy family, his story would read like a Horatio Alger saga. He was very tall and skinny as a youth with poor eyesight. He wanted to join an army, almost any army, but he was rejected for health reasons from the Austrian Army, the French Foreign Legion, and the British Forces for India. Had he been accepted he would have gone off to the wars and never heard from again, but that would not be his destiny. He was fluent in both German and French, but hadn't mastered English. Later in St. Louis in about 1868 at the Mercantile Library, where he had gone to work on his English, he came upon two gentlemen playing a game of chess while they conversed in German. He discreetly interjected himself in their conversation and game and all of a sudden, he was "discovered." They found him knowledgeable and charming beyond a man in his early 20's. They were the journalists for the German-language daily, the "Westiche Post" and they took Pulitzer under their wing, giving him a job in the newspaper business, and at age 25 he was offered controlling interest in the paper and he became a publisher.

In 1872 he bought the St. Louis Post for $3,000.00 and by 1878 he had purchased, for $2700.00, the St. Louis Dispatch, and combined the two papers as the St. Louis Post Dispatch. The same year he married Kate Davis in an Episcopal church. As an American citizen, editor and writer, he had mastered English and was a frequent speaker about town.

The term, "workaholic" hadn't been invented, but he was one. The clock had little meaning; working from early morning 'til past midnight was the rule. He was becoming wealthy. In 1883 he purchased the New York World. At that time it was about to be inundated by debts. He not only restored it, but built it into a force of some consequence, so much so that the publisher of a competitive New York paper resorted to personal attacks aimed at alienating the sizable Jewish population against him, "as a Jew that rejected his religion and heritage."

Even so, he was so colorful and innovative that his paper exuded his irrepressive ideas and style, and more growth and wealth followed him.

Of the many ironies in his life, one was that in the face of success he was going blind and had a hearing condition such that all but the most muffled noises caused him terrible pain. Another irony, "The Pulitzer Prizes," "given for journalistic excellence," was created by the originator of Yellow Journalism and the Yellow Kid. He and William Randolph Hurst, owner of the New York Journal, jousted one another in a "down and dirty" rivalry for greater circulation. Each vied with giant headlines and flamboyant "stories."

One of Pulitzer's best circulation promotions was to agree to a suggestion by a woman reporter, who's byline was "Nellie Bly." She had read Jules Vern's book, *"Around the World in Eighty Days,"* and the adventures of fictional hero, "Phileas Fogg." More than a million readers entered the NY World's contest when the publisher sent Nellie Bly out to circle the globe in less than 80 days, bettering the fictional Phileas, and invited his readers to guess the number of days, hours, minutes and seconds it would take her. The contest stimulated circulation greatly. When she returned in 72 days, 6 hours, 11 minutes and 14 seconds, she was greeted by huge crowds. The winner received a trip to Europe. She was bombastic and original, a muck-raker who exposed dire, dreadful conditions in sweat-shops, jails, insane asylums and government, writing first-hand accounts, after becoming, by different guises, a denizen of the institutions in question.

One more thing: the Statue of Liberty might still be stranded in France had not Pulitzer's New York World promoted public subscriptions to build the pedestal for it at the entrance to New York harbor.

Today Pulitzer Inc. founded by Joseph Pulitzer, owns 14 daily papers across the U.S. including the St. Louis Post-Dispatch and the Arizona Daily Star (Tucson). Also owns a string of weekly and biweekly community papers and a small stake in the St. Louis Cardinals baseball team. The Pulitzer family controls about 90% of the company.

"The power to mould the future of the Republic will be in the hands of the journalists of future generations." (Joseph Pulitzer.)

A Postscript: Although Pulitzer died in 1911, in 1913 one of the NY World editors, Arthur Wynne, concocted a puzzle he dubbed "word-cross" for a one time use. It was so popular that readers demanded more and more of them. The name now is "Crossword Puzzle".

CHAPTER FORTY-NINE

THE STRAUSES

IN MY ESTIMATION A MAJORITY of super-successful Jewish families emigrated from Bavaria, the Strauses among them. They came here in 1852. Bavaria was still an independent kingdom and didn't join Bismarck's 2nd Reich until 1871. The first Reich was the "Holy Roman Empire (962-1806)", which Napoleon destroyed in 1806. Napoleon's decree that all Jews take family names caused the patriarch Jacob Lazar to adopt the surname of Straus. Jacob's grandson Lazarus Straus (1809-1898) in 1852 brought the family to America. They settled in the South (Georgia). Later after the Civil War and hostilities were over, they moved to New York City. In Georgia he had been a successful merchant. His three sons, Isidor (1845-1912), Nathan (1848-1931) and Oscar (1850-1926) joined the father in the chinaware-glassware business in part for R. H. Macy and Company. Later in 1888 they bought into the company and by 1896 acquired full ownership.

The son Isidor, married, to Ida Blum, had four sons and three daughters. He served in the U.S. House of Representatives (1894-95) and was active in many charities. When he was 64 years of age on April 15, 1912, he and his wife were passengers on the S.S. Titanic. Both refused to take a place in the lifeboats so that "there would be more room for women and children." Also see "The Guggenheims." Benjamin (55 years old) died there too after giving his life jacket to a woman. Two years later a Straus progeny, Roger Williams Straus (1891-1957) married Gladys Eleanor Guggenheim. Roger William Straus eventually became president of ASARCO as defacto head of the massive

Guggenheim Metal Empire. He was a son of Oscar Solomon Straus.

Speaking of Oscar S. Straus, though early on he worked with his brothers Isidor and Nathan in the business, his great love was for public service. This youngest son of Lazarus was also a lawyer, and politically astute. He served in four different presidential administrations from Cleveland to Taft. He was the first American Ambassador to the Ottoman Empire. He helped Theodore Roosevelt compose a protest to the Russian government against their dreaded pogroms. He also communicated with Theodore Herzl who was the founder of the Zionist movement.

After Isidor's untimely death on the Titanic, his three surviving sons received his half of the business. It included Macy's and interest in the Department Store Holding Co., Abraham and Straus, etc. Nathan owned the other half. Isidor's sons did not agree with Nathan on many issues; soon they bought him out.

Though Nathan had left the business, he was far from retiring. He was a tireless pioneer for child welfare and public health. The beginning of the industrial age brought on challenges, especially in large cities like New York. During a bleak, cold winter he used his resources to provide food and coal during the economic plight 1892/93. The next winter he provided $2,000,000 of his funds for special "tickets," that were good for food, coal or shelter, all the while showing his concern for children's health. He demanded pasteurization of milk. Almost 25% of all babies born in New York City died before their first birthday. At his insistence a four-year pasteurization was tried on 20,000 babies. There were only 6 fatalities over 4 years. In 1920 at his expense he had opened nearly 300 milk depots in the U.S and abroad. His efforts brought pasteurization to most U.S. cities. At the turn of the century tuberculosis was rampant. He then created in Lakewood, N.J. a "T.B. Preventorium" for children. In 1911 President Taft appointed Nathan the only U.S.

delegate to an International Congress for the protection of the very young, that was held in Berlin, Germany. In another severe winter (1914—15) again he helped with food for those in need.

In their later years he and his wife established Child Health and Welfare Stations and Health Centers in Jerusalem and Tel Aviv for the benefit of all the inhabitants: Christians, Muslims and Jews. Arab rioting in 1929 broke their hearts. They both died shortly after 1930—31.

He certainly could have been listed among the Righteous Jews.

CHAPTER FIFTY

THE REICHMANNS

A FAMILY OF THE ULTRA-ORTHODOX Jews, from humble beginnings, escapes from Nazis. They become the fourth richest family in the world. Patriarch, "Samuel," born in Hungary 1898-1985 started their "roller-coaster" life, leaving Hungary fearing a Russian takeover, to Vienna, a Nazi hot-bed, to France, to Spain and Morocco and finally to Canada where their industry and energy would bring fabulous wealth, starting with the ceramic tile business, real estate and construction, and the building, managing, and owning of high-profile centers. Mired deep into the Cannery Wharf project at a time when vacancies outnumbered occupancies, bankruptcy awaited. Later they picked up the pieces, and finished it.

Their World Financial Center is severely damaged by the proximity to the World Trade Center. Wealth, power and orthodoxy did not immunize the family from perils, general and personal. For the family and for Samuel's sons, Edward, Louis, Albert, Paul and Ralph, their story is not at the beginning nor the end, but somewhere in between.

CHAPTER FIFTY-ONE

THE SELIGMANS

THE FOUNDER, JOSEPH (1829-1880) came from Baiersdorf, Bavaria. His father, David (1790-1845) was a weaver and a shopkeeper. Joseph, eldest of eight sons, was to be the founder of the International Banking House of J. and W. Seligman after he immigrated to the U.S. in 1837. At first he was a peddler, then expanded to dry goods shops in Lancaster, PA. then to Alabama and several locations throughout the country. He married a cousin and they had nine children; five were boys. It seems with a few exceptions that to have a successful business dynasty you should have a lot of sons and brothers.

With his successes, more members of his family joined him from Bavaria. During the booming gold rush in San Francisco the store there became involved in buying and selling gold, turning their retail merchandising into quasi-banking. During the Civil War they supplied clothing and supplies to the U. S. government. By the end of the war they had become international bankers. Some of the brothers established branches in New York, London and Frankfurt. Joseph was a trusted friend of President Ulysses S. Grant. He was active in fighting the corrupt, "Tweed –Ring" as a member of the Committee of 70" in New York. (A personal note: In 1946—47 when I was a student at the University of Pennsylvania I was an unpaid volunteer of the Philadelphia chapter of The Committee of Seventy.)

On religion, Joseph called himself a "free-thinker" but contributed time and money to the German Hebrew Orphan Asylum as well to other Jewish and non-Jewish charities.

CHAPTER FIFTY-TWO

BRIEF BRIEFS

Arisons (Ted)

"Ted" (1924-) founded Carnival Cruise Lines, emigrated from Israel in 1952 and has retired to live there.

Baruch (Bernard)

Best known as an advisor to both Democratic and Republican presidents. A wealthy but canny stock market speculator and noted philanthropist.

Bloomingdales (Family)

Department stores of same name, also some association with Broadway and Hollywood productions.

Blocks (Family)

H. & R. Block founded 1955

Crown, Henry

Henry – Chicago (1896-1990): Material Service, Real Estate, aerospace, General Dynamic Corp., Sports teams: Chicago White Socks, New York Yankees, Chicago Bulls, Charity, Jewish Theological Seminary.

Gimbels (Family)

Adam (1817-1896) Born in Bavaria, died in Philadelphia, PA. Chain of Department stores. More recently Peter Gimbel (1928-1987) undersea exploration.

Haases

Walter Abraham Sr. (1889-1979). Born in San Francisco. Long associated (through marriage) with Levi Strauss and family. Runs huge philanthropy with $600 million + to give away.

Blausteins

Louis (1864-1937) originally from Prussia. Son Jacob was founder of AMICO OIL CO., and was advisor to 5 U.S. Presidents.

Cohns

Alfred Einstein (1879-1957) New York City Physician, pioneer in electrocardiography. Edwin Joseph (1892-1953) New York City, a biochemist. Worked on large-scale methods of separating blood plasma into fractions. Was of great use for WWII wounded and still in use today.

Cohns (different family)

Jack (1889-1956) New York and Harry (1891-1958) New York. Pioneers in motion picture producers. Jack's son Robert (1920-1996) founded forerunner of Columbia Pictures.

CHAPTER FIFTY-THREE

THE LEHMANS

ANOTHER JEWISH DYNASTY OF over achievers coming out of Bavaria.

They arrived here in 1844 settling in Montgomery, Alabama opened a General Store, Lehman Brothers. In time "they," Henry (1821-1855), Emanuel (1827-1907) and Mayer (1830-1897) shifted their full energies to commodities trading, then a move to New York City becoming a successful, influential banking firm. Sons of the founding brothers also joined the enterprise. Mayer's sons, Irving (1876-1945) and Herbert (1878-1963) became famous by entering politics (Public Service). Herbert was FDR's Lt. Governor of New York state and became the Governor himself for four terms. During WWII he worked for the budding UN's Relief and Rehab. Organization. He had lost a son in WWII. In 1949 he became a U.S. Senator until 1957.

Brother Irving had married Sissie Straus, the daughter of Nathan Straus, an owner of Macy's Department stores. He became chief judge of the New York Court of Appeals, the state's highest court. He was an early "activist" judge. His liberal philosophy tended to extend his opinions beyond the intent of the legislatures that created them or even abrogate the statues as not constitutional to conform to his ideas of "social justice."

CHAPTER FIFTY-FOUR

THE TISCHES MEDIA CONNECTIONS

BROTHERS "LARRY" (LAWRENCE ALAN, 1923) and "Bob" (Preston Robert, 1926) both born in Brooklyn, New York. They created the Tisch Hotel chain, then bought into Loews Corp., a theater owner and management company and changed it into multi-faceted conglomerate that included: CNA Financial Corp, property, casualty, life and group insurance; Lorillard Inc. (Tobacco); Loews Hotels (18 of them); Diamond Offshore Drilling Co., (World's largest they own over 54%); Texas Gas Transmission LLC (5,800 miles of pipe); Bulova Corp.

In 1987 CBS communication complex face troubled times and Larry, who owned or controlled 24.9% of the stock, was voted president to bring it to profitability. He made some questionable moves, i.e. selling CBS Record subsidiary to Sony, the Japanese electronic giant and also selling off the Educational publishing division. Finally Westinghouse Electric agreed to purchase CBS.

The Tisch brothers gave millions to the Metropolitan Museum of Art and more millions to New York University.

CHAPTER FIFTY-FIVE

THE PRITZKERS

THE FAMILY EMIGRATED FROM Kiev Russia in 1881. The "to-be" patriarch was only 9 years old. On reaching maturity he had earned a law degree. His name was Nicholas Pritzker (1872-1957). He established a law firm, Pritzker and Pritzker in 1901. From then on all the family business from start to finish was filtered through it.

When Nicholas's sons Abram Nicholas Pritzker (1896-1986) and Jack Nicholas Pritzker (1904-1979) joined the firm their business ventures were so plentiful and successful that the law firm needed only one client. Abram had three sons who proved equally adept at expanding the family business. Jay Arthur Pritzker (1922-), Robert Alan Pritzker (1926-), and Donald Nicholas Pritzker (1932-1972). They acquired troubled companies at "fire-sale" prices and returned them to profitability. Much of these companies made up the "Marmon Group." At the same time the anchor, the premier enterprise, Hyatt hotels, was being brought to fore principally by Donald Nicholas Pritzker. Now the hotel chain consists of 207 hotels globally, and the Marmon Group is a 6 billion-a-year industrial conglomerate. Subsequent generations of the family have been and are active. The family up to now has shied away from going public, but the normally cohesive family consensus is stressed on different fronts. Fourth generation cousins clamor for a larger piece of the action; a saving and loan bank based in Hinsdale, Illinois, owned 50% by the Pritzkers, got in trouble; some $500 million FDIC insured funds were at risk. The Pritzker family in settling with

FDIC is indemnifying the deposits for the FDIC over a 15-year period and the institution, "Superior Bank" and branches have been sold off. Also the 9/11 incident has dampened the hotel occupancy and business in general.

CHAPTER FIFTY-SIX

LAUDER AND MORE

ESTÉE LAUDER, THE COMPANY NAME, there is a family behind it. Josephine Ester Mentzer (1908-1983) married Joseph Harold (Lauter) Lauder. The husband and wife team started selling skin cream formulated by her uncle to become the world's biggest, solely family-owned international beauty company. One of her sons who worked for the company took a leave of absence to become a U.S. Deputy Secretary of Defense and later ambassador to Austria, 1986-87 (Ronald Stephen Lauder).

Levitts

Abraham, New York (1880-1962) and sons built Levittowns in New York, Pennsylvania, New Jersey, Israel and elsewhere.

Mankiewiczes

Herman Jacob, (1897-1953) New York, journalist, playwright, screenwriter, i.e. Citizen Kane and others, along with skills of brother Joseph Leo and his sons and his brother's sons. One son of Herman, Frank Fabian, was president of National Public Radio.

Morgenthaus

Henry, born in Germany 1856, died in New York 1946, American Ambassador to Turkey, and his son Henry Jr. born N.Y. (1891-1969) was U. S. Secretary of the Treasury 1934-1945.

Ziffs

Another media family, founder William Bernard, 1898, Chicago, died 1953, N.Y. Ziff-Davis Publishing Co., periodicals Popular Flying, Popular Photograph, Radio News, Car and Driver, P.C. Mag., Stereo Review, Television stations until sold 1994 for 1.4 billion.

Selman Waksman

Born, Ukraine (1888-1973). In 1910 he emigrated to the U.S. He received undergraduate degree from Rutgers University and doctorate from University of California. In 1952 he received Nobel Prize for Psychology and Medicine and the discovery of antibiotic streptomycin. It became one of more important antibiotics due to its extensive effect on the greatest number of dangerous bacteria.

Jonas Salk

Born (1914) New York City, died 1995. Developed vaccine against polio. Later from the Salk Institute began the search for a vaccine to prevent AIDS.

John Von Neuman (1903-1957)

Born in Hungary. No doubt was a child prodigy. At age 6 he could converse in classical Greek. The son of a wealthy banker, and an extraordinary mathematician, he came to U.S. and helped in the atomic bomb project. He discovered how to detonate the bomb. It was his scheme that was the basis for, "store-intelligence" for computers that were to come.

Back to The Pequod

CHAPTER FIFTY-SEVEN

CAPT. GARDINER AND THE "RACHEL"

WHILE THE PEQUOD CREW from Ahab on down wanted to sight Moby Dick and all were intent on being first to see him, a large ship, though a whaler, came into view. It was the "Rachel." As it neared it was evident that most of its crew were top-side, and clustered by the gunwales. Their captain's boat was lowered and headed for the Pequod. While still a way off, Ahab bellows, "Hast seen the White-Whale?"

"Aye yesterday. Have ye seen a whale-boat adrift?"

Ahab answers in the negative. Soon the Rachel's skipper, Capt. Gardiner, comes aboard. He discloses that one of his four whale-boats had been separated and lost in gloom of the coming night. Further, that his 12-year-old son was one of the crew of that boat. Ahab recognizes Capt. Gardiner as a Nantucketer he knew. He made no move to initiate a salutary exchange. Instead he pried for more about the whale, "Where was he?" Not killed – not killed? How was it?" Capt. Gardiner relates his story to Ahab. The Rachel had put three boats out among a pod of whales and they were engaging them when Moby Dick appeared. It was then that the fourth boat, the best and fastest, was lowered and it raced into the fray, which was well out. It looked like they had made a contact with the white whale, but as sometimes happens, the whale may have run away with his pursuers, towing them out of sight.

Capt. Gardiner pleads with Ahab to help him in the search, but Ahab holds icy silence. He would even pay Ahab to cooperate in a concerted search for 48 hours. Capt. Gardiner couldn't imagine that Ahab would not be moved by his plea, but Ahab abruptly closes, "I will not do it. Even now I lose time. Good-bye...." Ahab goes below. The melancholy Capt. Gardiner makes his way back to his ship.

CHAPTER FIFTY-EIGHT

BOY SCOUTS OF AMERICA= SAD STORIES

STRANGELY SAD, THE FOLLOWING (excerpted from Washington Times, Jan. 15/21, 2001). Reform Jewish Leaders want to force The Boy Scouts of America to include homosexuals at all levels. (Their) Joint Commission for Social Order called on their 277 Boy Scout Chapters to disband and publicly protest the Boy Scout ban on homosexuals. The piece goes on to say, "...the boycott is one of many brought by the ruling of the U.S. Supreme Court that allows private organizations to set their own standards."

And again, though there is no religious organ involved, at the Democratic National Convention in Los Angeles, August 2000, when a half dozen invited Eagle Scouts mounted the stage, they were booed. These youngsters, had all qualified to be Eagles by maintaining personal fitness, community service and twenty-one merit badges, only to be heckled by "adults" because they were not "gay."

And the saddest of all: this story was told to me by a dear friend who lives a few blocks away. A woman of integrity and compassion, mother of four grown children with families of their own. Through her work in the health care field, she met a woman, a patient and a single parent with an 8-year-old son. He had been a "latch-key" child until our neighbor came into their lives. After that the boy began to enjoy sitting at a real family dinner table, among my friend's family, her husband (a colleague in health care), children and grandchildren and sometimes people like my wife and me. He now had a warm extended family and he could play and communicate with his peers there and at Sunday school (which she teaches). He had grown to regard our friend as a mother figure. His mom worked nights (in the entertainment business), and slept during the day. I don't know what trauma or other personal ordeal he may have suffered in the past. He was starved for affection, but he is active, inquisitive and itchy like boys his age. One evening when our friend was helping him with homework, he confided that his teacher (a male) told him that he must be "gay" and there was nothing he could do about it but "face it!" This upset the boy to find out that he'd been "consigned" by his teacher to follow that (his teacher's??) life style. Of course, our friend told him, "You're nothing of the kind! You are a real boy and don't let anyone say naught!"

Whom do we have teaching our children? What kind of misfits are their "advisors," "social workers," "psychologists??" New York city has already thrown-in-the-sponge, having a new high school devoted to young people who are or at least think they are homosexuals.

Maybe it is a fair idea to start a "segregation" program early? Prepare them for the Gay-Bars, Bath Houses, and AIDS in their future.

"Woe to those who call evil good, and good evil."

Isaiah 5:20

Mad Ahab is sure that Moby Dick represents, yea – causes evil. Ahab much like some Reform Jewish and Christian congregations that now embrace the new doctrines that coldly abandon much of the ancient truths, ethics and mores expressed in the Torah and Bible. They don't attach evil to one creature or a single source, but they abandon, degrade or even laugh at many expressions, parabolic stories of the Old and New Testament instead of probing for the secrets hidden within the written word. In place they now have "Media-Morality," the New Social Gospel that is "Politically Correct."

For all who are able to understand: We're here for just a short span, long enough however, to decide how we may spend eternity.

There are many examples of erosions in our hallowed institution, schools of higher learning; many colleges and universities have sunken to gutter levels with bogus ratiocinations. There is no right or wrong unless it pertains to hampering the exercise of "choice," for example, sexual preference.

All one has to do is to look at the Weimar Republic of pre-Nazi Germany. Decadence polluted much of that society, preparing it for Hitler's onslaught. There is an old medical aphorism, (largely ignored today) that goes, "You can't get a disease until you are sick." The disease organism is just hitting a pre-softened target or a prepared (fractured) moral economy that is ready to invite the next homicidal demigod who offers a "cure."

CHAPTER FIFTY-NINE

THE SHIP "DELIGHT" AND BURIAL AT SEA

AHAB NOW KNOWS THAT THE Pequod is near Moby Dick. He and Fedallah stay on deck constantly. Rarely speaking but forever watchful, Ahab decides that he'll be the first to sight the whale. He has Starbuck hoist him up the main-mast. Within ten minutes a black sea hawk with a red bill snatched Ahab's hat and flies off, dropping it in the ocean.

The Pequod sails on and days go by and another whaling ship draws near. It is "The Delight" and there in plain view on her "shears", the remains of a shattered, smashed whale-boat. Ahab calls across to her, "Hast seen the White Whale?"

The Delight captain replies by pointing to the wrecked whale-boat.

"Hast killed him?"

"The harpoon is not forged that will ever do that."

"Nantucketer; here in this hand I hold his death! Tempered in blood, and tempered by lightning are these barbs; and I swear to temper them triply in that hot place behind the fin, where the White Whale most feels his accursed life!"

Some of the Delight's crew are quietly engaged in sewing shut the mortal remains of their shipmate in his hammock. He expired from injuries sustained from yesterday's encounter with Moby Dick. Their captain goes on the say that this poor seaman is but one of four who met their fate battling the White Whale. He then orders the body to be committed to the sea as he intones, "...may the resurrection and the life..." The two ships were so close to each other that as the hammock clothed body is dropped the splash wets the Pequod's sides in spite of Ahab's quick but late orders to veer away.

Media's Sick Confederates

CHAPTER SIXTY

THE ACLU – AMERICAN CIVIL LIBERTIES UNION

THIS ORGANIZATION CLAIMS to be a "watch-dog" of the U.S. Constitution. Unfortunately it is permeated with lawyers who claim some genetic ties to Judaism. The thrust of their philosophy is to suffocate any sublime words of wisdom for fear that they may have a religious origin.

Their strident position is the routing out of any expression of faith, be it remote or direct, but in so doing they too are proffering a religion – Atheism.

The Ten Commandments given by God to Moses are similar to the Fountain Head of Laws found in many cultures from the ancient world. Within them one can find the basis of all civilized law. They are not tenets of one religion, yet the ACLU has been successful in having them removed in several locations. I understand they want the words, "Under God," extracted from our Pledge of Allegiance and, "In God We Trust," taken from our coins."

The ACLU protests that what they are doing is for our own good. They know what's best for our own good. I guess most of us are pretty stupid. We need the ACLU to figure things out. Don't we?

Along with that the ACLU has used its legal muscle to defend the Child-molester Group "NAMBLA," (North American Man Boy Love Association). Two pedophiles, members of the group, brutally raped and murdered a ten-year-old boy.

The boy's family has sued the North American Man Boy Love Association for wrongful death. The two men picked up the 5th grader, took him to The Boston Public Library where the NAMBLA's website was accessed. Later when attempting a sexual assault, the child, Jeffrey Curley, fought back, but they gagged him with a gasoline-soaked rag and later killed him. They then put his body in a tub with concrete and threw it in a river.

The ACLU wanted the suit against NAMBLA dismissed as, "Unconstitutional."

The ACLU doesn't want any crosses or religions symbols displayed on government property. I wonder how long it will take them to remove all the crosses and Stars of David from our National Cemeteries?

Received on the Internet:

I've excerpted only a small portion of the following:

Darrell Scott, the father of Rachel Scott, a victim of the Columbine High School shootings in Littleton, Colorado, was invited to address the House Judiciary Committee's subcommittee. What he said to our national leaders during this special session of Congress was painfully truthful.

"*I am here today to declare that Columbine was not just a tragedy – it was a spiritual event that should be forcing us to look at where the real blame lies! Much of the blame lies here in this room. Much of the blame lies behind the pointing fingers of the accusers themselves. I wrote a poem just four nights ago that expresses my feelings best. This was written way before I knew I would be speaking here today.*"

> *Your laws ignore our deepest needs,*
> *You words are empty air.*
> *You've stripped away our heritage,*
> *You've outlawed simple prayer.*
> *Now gunshots fill our classrooms,*
> *And precious children die.*
> *You seek for answers everywhere,*
> *And ask the question, "Why?"*
> *You regulate restrictive laws,*
> *Through legislative creed.*
> *And yet you fail to understand,*
> *That God is what we need!*

CHAPTER SIXTY-ONE

LINCOLN'S DECLARATION OF THANKSGIVING AS A NATIONAL HOLIDAY, 1863

RX: READ ALOUD. *It is the duty of nations as well as of men to owe their dependence upon the overruling power of God; to confess their sins and transgressions in humble sorrow, yet with assured hope that genuine repentance will lead to mercy and pardon; and to recognize the sublime truth, announced in the Holy Scriptures and proven by all history, that those nations are blessed whose God is the Lord.*

We know that by His divine law, nations, like individuals, are subjected to punishments and chastisements in this world. May we not justly fear that the awful calamity of civil war which now desolates the land may be a punishment inflicted upon us for our presumptuous sins, to the needful end of our national reformation as a whole people?

We have been the recipients of the choicest bounties of heaven, we have been preserved these many years in peace and prosperity' we have grown in numbers, wealth and power as no other nation has ever grown.

But we have forgotten God. We have forgotten the gracious hand which preserved us in peace and multiplied and enriched and strengthened us, and we have vainly imagined, in the deceitfulness of our hearts, that all these blessings were produced by some superior wisdom and virtue of our own.

Intoxicated with unbroken success, we have become too self-sufficient to feel the necessity of redeeming and reserving grace, too proud to pray to the God that made us.

It has seemed to me fit and proper that God should be solemnly, reverently and gratefully acknowledged as with one heart and one voice, by the whole American people. I do therefore invite my fellow citizens in every part of the United States, and also who are at sea and those who are sojourning in foreign lands, to set apart and observe the last Thursday of November as a Day of Thanksgiving and praise to our beneficent Father who dwelleth in the heavens.

(signed) A. Lincoln
October 3, 1863

CHAPTER SIXTY-TWO

THE FIRST DAY

IT IS EVENING. AHAB IS ON DECK. Suddenly he grips the near pinrail, becomes motionless, like a hunting dog, he sniffs the air and declares that a whale must be near. He then deduces its bearing by the odor, then orders the ship's course to be slightly changed and the sail shortened. At daybreak his actions are vindicated. There is evidence of cetacean presence; a long sleek on the sea, smooth as oil, like polished metal, a contrast to the restless ocean and a signature of a great whale submerged and moving.

Ahab decides to go aloft again. As he is hoisted to a vantage place between the main-top-sail and the top-gallant-sail, he spots the white whale and cries, "There she blows – there she blows!" "A hump like a snow hill, it is Moby Dick!" Seamen that were also watching for whales claimed that they too had seen Moby Dick at almost the same time. Ahab says, "Not at the same instant, not the same, no, the doubloon is mine."

The boats are lowered, and the chase is about to begin. Ahab's passing words to Starbuck, "...remember, stay on board and keep the ship." All the boats but Starbucks had been dropped and the boat sails set, with all the paddlers plying.

Great whales over the eons, well before man's emergence, had few natural enemies. Those they had, they evolved ways of dealing with. With "man," could these small, inconsequential, unnatural "things" be a threat? For the sperm whale, after hunting and battling and dining on giant squid, would come to the surface to lounge and relax, taking little care that surface creatures drew near other than to curiously observe them. In a sense, let the strange creatures kill them. Early on, they didn't regard their presence as a threat that left themselves open to be exploited as a "commodity" and killed. I wonder if there is a message there vis-à-vis the media and its curious viewers, readers and listeners. In any event, Moby Dick was different; he perceived man as a threat and he fought back.

Ahab's boat seemed to have been singled out by Moby Dick. The first indication was the birds; they were flying, single-file towards Ahab's boat, following the submerged whale using their extraordinary eyesight. When they flew just above Ahab's boat their precision flight broke up and they began to flutter and circle about. At this time Ahab peered down into the depths and saw, a white living spot, "deep down that appeared to be growing as he viewed it until two long rows of white glistening teeth floated up from the "undiscoverable bottom." It was Moby Dick's open mouth. Now Ahab was in the tantalizing vicinity of his foe, but helpless at the very jaws of his nemesis. Anticipating this possibility earlier, he took the Perth harpoon from Fedallah and changed places with Fedallah at the bow so that he'd be ready to thrust the weapon into the whale, but Moby Dick suddenly changed his position and took the bow portion of the boat in his jaws, coming within six inches of Ahab's head, causing havoc among the crew. Fedallah alone showed no emotion. The stout gunwales ruptured and splintered. The craft had been bitten in two. The whale moved off. Ahab was in the water and the crew clung to the two halves of the boat. Meanwhile the whale was "pitchpoling" - lurching his great body 20 or more feet into the air, shortly to resume his aggressive, horizontal attitude and started making circles around the wreck and the whale-boat crew. Ahab was yet in the water. The Pequod, under Starbuck's guidance, sails between the whale and the struggling sailors. Moby Dick suddenly swims off. The two undamaged boats flew to the rescue. Ahab's first words to the rescuers, "The harpoon... is it safe?"

"Aye, sir, for it was not darted; this is it."

"Lay it before me; any missing men?" All five men had survived. Ahab then orders the remaining whale-boat people, including the recent de-boated crew to double-bank the oars (two men to each position) but the whale was plainly out distancing their efforts, so they returned to the Pequod. Ahab did not rest nor would anyone. They followed the whale, noting his every spouting. Ahab commanded to be lifted to his perch and then again to the deck, continuing until it became too dark to see and report the spoutings.

Ahab gives orders for the night's vigil, keeping a slower pace, but maintaining the direction. He then advances toward the doubloon in the main-mast and says, "Men, this gold is mine, for I earned it; but I shall let it abide here till the White-Whale is dead; and then whosoever of ye first raises, upon the day he shall be killed, this gold is that man's; and if on that day I shall again raise him, then ten times it's sum shall be divided among all of ye! Away now! (To the mate says), The deck is thine, Sir."

CHAPTER SIXTY-THREE

NEIL POSTMAM

Messianics, etc.

I N THE PANTHEON OF HIGH ACHIEVING Jews you can include Neil Postman. He died October 5, 2003, as holy Yom Kippur was to begin. He was a professor at New York University, the author of several books on media: *"Entertaining Ourselves to Death"* and others. His main theme is warnings of latent poisons that go into the media mix as we're receiving them. He also cites two 20th century sentinel authors and their seminal works: George Orwell's *"1984"* and Aldous Huxley's *"Brave New World."*

In Orwell's *1984* we will be oppressed by "Big Brother's" rigid micro-management of our lives to the point where even mundane choices are made for us. Achieving maturity is thwarted, books are banned, history is altered and we end up as captives of the controllers of information.

He goes on to Huxley's *Brave New World (Revisited)* as quite the opposite. Orwell writes of external oppression and pain to bring about in the *1984* nightmare but not in the Huxley work. No books are banned, instead they are deluged with material written, spoken and viewed. Everyone is drowned in a sea of irrelevance.

Orwell feared that we'd be a captive culture. Huxley feared that we would be a trivial culture. In *1984* people are controlled by inflicting pain. In Huxley's *Brave New World*, people are controlled by inflicting "pleasure."

Professor Postman tends to side with Huxley's view. He is correct in part, but Orwell's proposition is valid too. True, the real 1984 has come and gone and we haven't noticed the pain, but certainly some of _1984's_ aura has broached our shores and the controls are being applied in political correctness, and books are "banned" by selective featuring – promoting only those that are "acceptable." Our history isn't exactly being rewritten. It is not being taught and if it sees light at all, it is slanted for "P.C." and the teacher's prejudices. The reputation of historic heroes are being sullied and down-graded in favor of Black History or Gay Lifestyle.

The awful results of the above have been demonstrated several times. A TV show host asks almost juvenile history questions to adult men and women, on-the-street such as, "Who was our first president?" Answer given: Lincoln and Roosevelt, and what country did we fight in Europe in World War II?" Answer: Russia. There were more inane answers.

The above author's works have been prophetic. We are covertly oppressed and we can "Entertain Ourselves to Death" and we love our oppressors.

Here are two Neil Postman quotes to remember:

1. "You can evaluate the meaning of a sentence and say, no to it. You can't say no to a picture."

2. "Children are the living messengers we send, to a time we will not see."

Is Dr. Postman an anomaly? Jews are dominant in media/ entertainment, yes and even porn. The Torah: Jews are commanded to be a holy nation, a kingdom of priests. Can they yet be a force in all levels of pornography? Are they Jews in name only? Some say most U.S. Jews are secular, actually ignorant of what their religion teaches and are kept that way by Reform Rabbis. There are movements effecting Jews not satisfied with the status quo. Some are gravitating towards Orthodox Judaism; others maintaining Jewish ritual and traditions are now called

Messianic Jews. It is a worldwide movement that supports the state of Israel and feels The Advent a fulfillment of the Prophecies of the Tanach (Old Testament). They worship Yeshua (Jesus) but continue to keep much of the Jewish symbols, Star of David, menorah, etc. They have congregations in almost every state, and Canada, Israel, Austria, Argentine, Australia, Belgium, Brazil, Columbia, Costa Rica, El Salvador, France, Germany, Great Britain, Guatemala, Holland, Mexico, New Zealand, Russia, Paraguay, Puerto Rico, Spain, Ukraine, Venezuela. In addition there are Christian places of worship (churches) sharing their facilities in more states and Canada, and internationally. The movement has about 300 congregations in the U.S and Canada and 24 congregations in Israel, and more throughout the world. They have synagogues, and their priests are called Rabbis. They celebrate Rosh Hashanah, Yom Kippur, use of the Shofar, etc.

The Messianics point out that modern Reform Jews make the five books of Moses irrelevant to their faith, noting their stand on homosexuality. Messianics further accept most of the Maimonides, (13 principles of faith) where most American Jews will not.

They are accused by other bodies of Jews of being "Christians." They maintain they're not, but are Messianic Jews. Their movement is growing. One figure stated that they outnumber Reform Jews in Israel.

The dominant power bases in Jewry contend, "You can't be a Jewish/Christian." The Messianics reply in effect, "Is it okay to be a Jewish/Atheist or a Jewish/Homosexual?"

There are other Jewish/Christian consociations similar to the Messianics that are growing.

The Jewish Diaspora may be looked on as a tribulation that will never end until the Jews return to their "home." In providence perhaps their protracted odyssey and suffering has unconsciously enabled them to make worldwide contributions. In all places they had ventured and settled, they enriched the countries with their cultural, scientific, humane, and business energies and at times their seeds. They look to return to that Land Flowing with Milk and Honey, yet it is close, so close. Is it within them?

CHAPTER SIXTY-FOUR

THE SECOND DAY

THE MAST-HEADS WERE manned at first light. Whale ship captains knew that at nightfall a whale already had its bearings for the dark, possibly set by a navigational intelligence unknown to man or by seeing coastal landmarks. In any event at night they usually traveled in straight lines. Of course Ahab knew this, but the wind and the seas are either his allies or enemies in following in the dark.

All the crew now seemed to embrace this singular enterprise to find and kill Moby Dick. There was a corporate oneness of the crew and ship, "The hand of fate had snatched all their souls ... that unseen agency which so enslaved them to the race." After one false sighting, Moby Dick revealed himself with a thunderous and spectacular breaching into the air. His act of defiance! Challenge?

Ahab cries, "aye, breach your last to the sun, Moby Dick, thy hour and thy harpoon are at hand!"...Then to the boats, "Mr. Starbuck, the ship is thine – keep away from the boats, but keep near them. Lower all!"

Little time intervened before Moby Dick confronted the three boats. The White Whale burst into furious speed, rushing among them, open jaws and lashing tail, heedless of the irons being darted at him from every boat, his power could reduce them to match-wood. In the chaos that follows, Flask and Stubb's boats are destroyed. Ahab is nearly killed in the tangle of line attached to harpoons and lances which he manages to cut free just as the whale capsizes his boat. In the melee Ahab's whale-bone leg is snapped off. Again the Pequod under Starbuck comes to the rescue, picking up the sprained and wounded mariners and what hardware, lances, harpoons, rope and boat parts could be found. From the keel of Ahab's wrecked boat, the ship's carpenter began to fashion a new leg for him.

Ahab calls a muster. All hands are accounted for except one, the Parsee-Fedallah. "The Parsee!" cried Stubb, he must have been caught in..." Ahab refused to believe that the Parsee is gone. He orders that the ship be searched. He cannot be found.

"Aye, Sir," said Stubb, "caught among the tangles of your lines – I thought I saw him dragging under." Ahab is shaken and Starbuck vents his pent-up bile, "Great God! But for one single instant show thyself, never, never wilt thou capture him old man – In Jesus' name, no more of this, that's worse than devil's madness. Two days chased; twice stove to splinters; thy very leg once more snatched from under thee ... shall we chase this murderous fish till he swamp the last man? ..."

Ahab's guru confidant has drowned, ensnared in Ahab's own lines, and his prophecy that he would not die until Fedallah had gone first crosses his mind. His response to Starbuck is cryptic, "This whole act (is) immutably decreed, 'twas rehearsed by thee and me a billion years before this ocean rolled. Fool! I am Fate's lieutenant! I act under orders...Look you thou, underling! That thou obeyest mine ..."

He then rallies the men to continue, saying that on the morrow Moby Dick "he'll rise once more – but only to spout his last!"

"D'ye feel brave men, brave?"

"As fearless fire," cried Stubb.

The men go forward, Ahab mutters to himself, "The things called omens! ...The Parsee – the Parsee – gone – gone? And he was to go before – but still was to be seen again ere I could perish – How's that? There's a riddle ... I'll solve it though!"

When dusk came on, the whale was still in sight. Again the sail was shortened, only the sound of hammers and the hum of the grind-stone was heard as men toiled by lanterns preparing the spare boats and weapons for a fresh battle tomorrow.

Contending with the vagaries of wind, currents, and the whale's unfathomable fiendish power, Ahab finally has him in a battle-theatre. But Moby Dick despoils him again and again.

Now Ahab marshals all his resources for yet another encounter.

But before that, consider:

CHAPTER SIXTY-FIVE

THE PROTOCOLS OF THE LEARNED ELDERS OF ZION & VIETNAM

PERHAPS SOME OF TODAY'S JEWS are subliminally stressed by the centuries of pogroms, exclusions, and depredations, and subtle and blatant discriminations. For the most part they no longer exist, yet are they really gone? There are factors at work to re-ignite them, active and passive.

Could the valorous, "Zion-Experiment" (The State of Israel) be at the seat of present "Islamic" (not just Palestine) atrocities? Of course, their aim in terrorizing is to finger Jews as the source of our discommodation.

But some (lots) of homegrown media types push too far, under the cover of "entertainment" and the First Amendment. Covertly they destroy the things that bombs can't reach, the moral consensus and decency.

Recently I heard of a "ruling" from the FCC (Federal Communications Commission) Deputy General Counsel David H. Solomon's libertine decision to now call the "F" word's use as just another adjective. Bit by bit an enervation of the efforts to eliminate prejudice will surely bring back "the good old days." (FCC Order File #EB-03-iH-0110)*

Within a week of discovering this, I found that FCC Chairman Michael Powell was moved to rethink the "F" word use. The FCC was inundated with thousands of letters and e-mails, thanks to the American Family Association, Parents Television Counsel, Cuss Control Academy and others protesting the ruling.

However there are still exceptions in the electronic media regarding "blue" language.

The "good old days" produced such "classical" writings, as *The Protocols of the Learned Elders of Zion*. I started reading them. They're laborious, an interminable insult to the intelligence of any would-be real Jewish conspirators. Hitler bought and referred to them in *Mein Kampf*. Henry Ford in his time was no "closet" anti-Semite. He owned a newspaper, the Dearborn Independent, in which he published, and even serialized, versions of them. Actually their origins go back to the 18th century, supposedly about a Masonic plot to rule the world. It was written to discredit, to throttle, the growing political influence of the Masons. Years later, they were plagiarized, with few changes. Jews were substituted for Masons. It has been in this form since the 19th century and it is still being circulated.

On Henry Ford's death the company did an about face. To maintain their image as one of the Free World's manufacturing colossus they didn't need, nor want, Henry's anti-Semitic baggage. It appears they went out of their way to dispel even a hint of slighting or degrading minorities. They bent backwards in hiring politically liberal management teams. Robert McNamara, a graduate of Berkeley, with a graduate degree form Harvard, became Ford's first non-family member president in 1960. Less than a month as the Ford company president, he became President Kennedy's Secretary of Defense. He brought with him his own Berkeley honed baggage. The appointment was a titanic mistake. There is evidence that the Liberal theme prevailed and the armed services became a platform for Social Engineering during the Vietnam Catastrophe.

Aside from tactical blunders that wasted the lives of our fighting men and our treasure in that conflict, there were other stupid, dreadful decisions made. I've talked with field officers, now retired, who spoke of an aspect of that, that the media never covered. They told me of receiving recruits by the truckloads who were found to be dregs, illiterate and or dope-pushers, car thieves, hold-up men, pimps, etc.

In each case they had "elected" (plea-bargained) to go into the Armed Services instead of jail. The innocent "Inductee" boy-next-door was thrown in with them on the specious theory that his presence and life-style would reform or ameliorate their proclivity for crime. What really happened was an explosion of narcotic use and destructive-anarchistic behavior that has infected our subsequent generations and costing untold billions and deaths (from OD's and "Friendly Fire") Fresh body bags are still being counted.

So much for the Protocols of the Elders of Zion.

Further there are enough soft-headed citizens who are looking for someone or something to blame for the sorry conditions and they readily join the likes of skin-heads, Neo-Nazis, Aryan Nations, White Pride, The Ku Klux Klan, etc. The Klan has even set up chapters in Britain and Australia. And according to the September 25th, 2000 issue of U.S. News and World Report, the Internet helps build a sophisticated web of violent, well-funded racists.

CHAPTER SIXTY-SIX

THE THIRD DAY

THE MORNING DAWNED "fair and fresh." Every mast-head carried lookouts, even out to the spars.

"D'ye see him?" Ahab calls. The whale was not in sight. The day, the weather, a fairer day could not have occurred. Ahab doesn't dwell on it but cries, "Aloft there! What d'ye see?"

"Nothing Sir."

"Nothing!" and it is almost noon. See the sun, I've over-sailed him. Aye, he's chasing me now, not I him – that's bad ... Come about! Come down all of ye, but the regular lookouts! Man the braces."

Starbuck maintaining his restraint, murmurs to himself, "God, keep us ... I obey my God in obeying him!"

"Stand by to sway me up!" Ahab advances toward the hempen basket. "We should meet him soon."

"Aye, aye sir," and Starbuck did.

After an hour Ahab notes a spout again and the other lookouts sound off in chorus. The boats are about to be lowered. Ahab briefly considered the Parsee's riddle, "What's that he said? He should still go before me, my pilot; and yet to be seen again? But where? Will I have eyes at the bottom of the sea?..."

"Starbuck!" Ahab calls as his boat is about to be lowered.

"Sir," Starbuck answers. Ahab offers his hand and Starbuck weeps and makes one more plea to give up the chase. Ahab tosses his arm from him, "Lower away."

A voice was heard as the boat was pulling round close under the stern. "The sharks! The sharks!" came a voice from the low cabin window. "O master, my master, come back!" Was it Pip? The sharks did "maliciously" snap at the oar-blades each time they dipped in the water.

Starbuck on the Pequod shudders as a depression cloud sweeps his heart and mind, thinking of his wife and children. He shakes it off and is back to controlling the ship, "Aloft there – keep thy keenest eye upon the boats; mark well the whale ..."

Ahab in his boat headed for the whale again mulls over the Parsee's prophecy, "No coffin and no hearse can be mine – and hemp only can kill me! Ha! Ha!"

Suddenly out of the depths Moby Dick sounded, shooting up into the air and crashing back causing a rainbowed mist that hung in the air as though it was part of the performance.

Ahab orders the boats on the attack, but Moby Dick with fresh iron in him from yesterday's encounter came churning his tail among the boats emptying two of them of all their weapons and damaging them. Ahab's boat was intact and while moving around the three boats, the crews and Ahab could see lashed round and round the whale's back reeled lines and pinioned under the turns was the body of Fedallah the Parsee. Ahab dropped the harpoon from his hand. And Ahab cries, "Aye Parsee, I see thee again. – Aye and thou goest before and this then is the hearse that thou didst promise. But where is the second hearse?"

He then tells the crews of the damaged boats to return to the Pequod and try to repair the boats and return to the chase if possible. Ahab would continue and came close enough to the Pequod to order Starbuck to follow him. Starbuck again implores him to desist saying, "See! Moby Dick seeks thee not. It is thou that madly seekest him!"

Ahab persisted and finally was within the mist of its last spouting. Ahab poised and, "darted his fierce iron, and his far fiercer curse into the hated whale."

The whale then crashes into the ship causing fatal damage and massive water intake. Ahab is still in his whaleboat nearby and cries, "The ship! The hearse! – The second hearse! Its wood could only be American." Ahab, the ship and the whale are all close. Ahab's harpoon was darted and the whale flew with great velocity and the line attached to the harpoon became fouled and as Ahab tried freeing it, it caught him round the neck and he shot out of the boat and was gone in an instant. The line "rope" is made of hemp.

As the Pequod sinks, a great whirlpool occurs, pulling everything including the lone boat under. Everyone perishes except one, Ishmael, who lives to tell the story.

"And I only am escaped alone to tell thee."

...Job

Ishmael survives because he was tossed from the whaleboat before it became close to the Pequod. The vortex of the whirlpool was spent by the time the suction had pulled him to its axis and the coffin/life-buoy shot up from the depth and floated by his side. He rested on it for a day and a night. The second day a sail drew near and a ship picked him up. It was the Rachel still looking for, "her missing children, but only found another orphan."

Its skipper Capt. Gardiner exercises his Christian duty and rescues the "orphan.

CHAPTER SIXTY-SEVEN

JEWS, CHRISTIANS, MUSLIMS AND OTHERS

AMERICAN CHRISTIANS, DEFENDERS of Israel read in their Bibles that Israel, The Promised Land was promised to the Jews: God-inspired Jews who follow strict diet laws, honor the Sabbath and are bound by stern codes for sexual behavior. What is seen on TV doesn't show a semblance of the Jews of The Bible. On the contrary, they're filling the programming with violence, sexual content, subtle, blatant and perverse.

TV makes Jews the least religious of the American population. Serious Christians wonder, "Where are the Jews of The Bible to whom the land was promised, where are they?"

Questions are aroused between Jews of today and those of The Bible by the indifference of modern Jews to the "sanctity" of the land.

In a recent survey of the Jewish Studies Center CCNY they conclude, *"that of the 5.5 million Americans defined by sociologists as Jewish, half list their religion as "other" or "none."*

Conservative Christians are disillusioned with the behavior and attitude of Jews towards porn and ethics. Up to now they have been the Jews' strongest allied group.

The loss of the consensus of the revealed truths as pronounced by Judeo/Christian ethics can and has resulted in producing unbridled conscienceless fiends such as Hitler, Stalin, Pol Pot and even a minor commander of a small Pacific island group during WWII where this Japanese officer had served at his mess (dinner) a paté made from the livers of murdered American flyers. He was hanged as a war criminal.

There are profound demographic stats that war with the Judeo/Christian epoch.

Worldwide, the Jewish population is estimated to be 13 to 14 million. Israel has 5.5 to 6 million and the U.S. has about the same amount, or for the two about 11 or 12 million. That leaves only around 2.5 to 3 million for all of the rest of the world. As noted before, many are Jews in name only. Further, 30% of married Jews have non-Jewish spouses. Also many are Messianic Jews.

On the other hand, the Islamic World population is near 1.9 billion. In the Near East alone (mostly Arabs) there are about 133 million living in 22 countries. They're increasing in all parts of the world. In Europe their increase is 142% (1998). Islam is the second largest religious group in France, Great Britain and the U.S.A. (Muslims in the USA are 10 million and Jews 5.5 to 6 million.)

If those figures aren't enough to scare this tiny sliver of the 6 billion world population, then consider a new onslaught coming not from hostiles, but from the world's largest ethnic population, the Asians. Isolate their emergence in the U.S.A. They are not hostile. There is not a religious component that could contest the Jews, but what they have that is similar or even more pronounced than the Jews: the intense love of knowledge, of achieving scholastically, a deep cultural heritage, ability to adapt and a strong work ethic and family cohesiveness and in many a "race" memory, i.e. not dishonoring by their behavior those that came before. This last was strong with Jews of old, but not too evident any more. Also, along with all of the above they have the discipline to put these gifts to use. Another way of expressing this might be: We are now seeing their Genies emerge from those ancient bottles where severe insular governments, old taboo and geography held the caps on.

Will they supplant the Jews in creative, cultural and mercantile energy? They may very well do it in time to the whole society. They have already secured many beachheads and for the most part are being welcomed. In media, Larry Tische sold the CBS Record subsidiary to Sony. Of course, there are many products made by Japanese that are household names beside the automobiles, trucks, electronics, etc., but for the most part the Japanese have the smallest of numbers of the Asian population that are permanent U.S. residents and it declined by 6% but all the rest, some 10.2 million have had a 48% increase since 1990.

> Note: CHINESE: 3.8 MILLION
> FILIPINO: 3.2 MILLION
> ASIAN INDIAN: 2.8 MILLION
> VIETNAMESE: 1.7 MILLION
> KOREAN: 1.6 MILLION
> JAPANESE: 1.3 MILLION

Most of the Korean, Filipino, and Vietnamese are Christians and portions of the Chinese and some Japanese are also. So the old and new testaments will still influence our cultures in the future.

Perhaps only a remnant of the extraordinary "chosen people" will be with us. The Babylonians, Assyrians, Romans, and Hitlers failed, but the "final solution" belongs to the Jews of Hollywood.

"...you shall be left few in number, whereas you were as the stars in heaven in multitude..." Deuteronomy 28-62.

Capt. Gardiner found a remnant floating in a great sea atop a coffin.

Printed in the United States
By Bookmasters